A
Shropshire
Christmas

Compiled by Lyn Briggs

ALAN SUTTON

First published in the United Kingdom in 1993
Alan Sutton Publishing Limited · Phoenix Mill · Far Thrupp
Stroud · Gloucestershire

First published in the United States of America in 1993
Alan Sutton Publishing Inc · 83 Washington Street · Dover
NH 03820

British Library Cataloguing in Publication Data
A catalogue record for this book is available from the
British Library

ISBN 0 7509 0098 9

Library of Congress Cataloging in Publication Data
applied for

Cover picture: The High Street, Shrewsbury *by E. Hay*
(photograph: Bridgeman Art Library)

Typeset in 12/13 Garamond.
Typesetting and origination by
Alan Sutton Publishing Limited.
Printed in Great Britain by
Redwood Books, Trowbridge, Wiltshire

Contents

from

The Raven in the Foregate

ELLIS PETERS

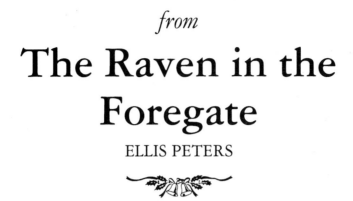

Brother Cadfael is a popular hero in Shropshire. Created by novelist Ellis Peters, he is a Benedictine monk who lives in Shrewsbury Abbey where he grows herbs and solves crimes. The Raven in the Foregate, *the twelfth chronicle in the series, is set at Christmas in 1141 against a background of civil unrest as King Stephen and Empress Maud struggle for the crown. It concerns the murder on Christmas Eve of an unloved parish priest.*

Hugh was gone, riding south for Canterbury in uncustomary state, well escorted and in his finery. He laughed at himself, but would not abate one degree of the dignity that was his due. 'If I come back deposed,' he said, 'at least I'll make a grand departure, and if I come back sheriff still, I'll do honour to the office.'

After his going Christmas seemed already on the doorstep, and there were great preparations to be made for the long night vigil and the proper celebration of the Nativity, and it was past Vespers on Christmas Eve before Cadfael had time to make a brief visit to the town, to spend at least an hour with

Aline, [Hugh's wife] and take a gift to his two-year-old godson, a little wooden horse that Martin Bellecote the master-carpenter had made for him, with gaily coloured harness and trappings fit for a knight, made out of scraps of felt and cloth and leather by Cadfael himself.

A soft, sleety rain had fallen earlier, but by that hour in the evening it was growing very cold, and there was frost in the air. The low, moist sky had cleared and grown infinitely tall, there were stars snapping out in it almost audibly, tiny but brilliant. By the morning the roads would be treacherous, and the frozen ruts a peril to wrenched ankles and unwary steps. There were still people abroad in the Foregate, most of them hurrying home by now, either to stoke up the fire and toast their feet, or to make ready for the long night in church. And as Cadfael crossed the bridge towards the town gate, the river in full, silent dark motion below, there was just enough light left to put names to those he met, coming from their shopping laden and in haste to get their purchases home. They exchanged greetings with him as they passed, for he was well known by his shape and his rolling gait even in so dim a light. The voices had the ring of frost about them, echoing like the chime of glass.

And here, striding across the bridge towards the Foregate, just within the compass of the torches burning under the town gate, came Ralph Giffard, on foot. Without the sidelong fall of the torchlight he would not have been recognized, but thus illuminated he was unmistakable. And where could Giffard be going at this time of the evening, and out of the town? Unless he meant to celebrate Christmas at the church of Holy Cross instead of in his own parish of Saint Chad. That was possible, though if so he was over-early. A good number of the wealthier townsfolk would also be making for the abbey this night.

Cadfael went on up the long curve of the Wyle, between the sparkling celestial darkness and the red, warm, earthy

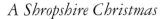

Snow, frost and ice add a fairy-tale quality to this photograph of
Shrewsbury

torchlight, to Hugh's house close by Saint Mary's church, and
in through the courtyard to the hall door. No sooner had he
set foot within than the excited imp Giles bore down upon
him, yelling, and embraced him cripplingly round the thighs,
which was as high as he could reach. To detach him was easy
enough.

As soon as the small, cloth-wrapped parcel was lowered
into his sight he held up his arms for it gleefully, and
plumped down in the rushes of the hall floor to unwrap it
with cries of delight. But he did not forget, once the first
transports were over, to make a rush for his godfather again,
and clamber into his lap by the fireside to present him with a

moist but fervent kiss in thanks. He had Hugh's self-reliant nature, but something also of his mother's instinctive sweetness.

'I can stay no more than an hour,' said Cadfael, as the boy scrambled down again to play with his new toy. 'I must be back for Compline, and very soon after that begins Matins, and we shall be up all the night until Prime and the dawn Mass.'

'Then at least rest an hour, and take food with me, and stay until Constance fetches my demon there away to his bed. Will you believe,' said Aline, smiling indulgently upon her offspring, 'what he says of this house without Hugh? Though it was Hugh told him what to say. He says he is the man of the house now, and asks how long his father will be away. He's too proud of himself to miss Hugh. It pleases his lordship to be taking his father's place.'

'You'd find his face fall if you told him longer than three or four days,' said Cadfael shrewdly. 'Tell him he's gone for a week, and there'll be tears. But three days? I daresay his pride will last out that long.'

At that moment the boy had no attention to spare for his dignity as lord of the household or his responsibilities as its protector in his father's absence, he was wholly taken up with galloping his new steed through the open plain of rushes, on some heroic adventure with an imaginary rider. Cadfael was left at liberty to sit with Aline, take meat and wine with her, and think and talk about Hugh, his possible reception at Canterbury, and his future, now hanging in the balance.

'He has deserved well of [King] Stephen,' said Cadfael firmly, 'and Stephen is not quite a fool, he's seen too many change their coats, and change them back again when the wind turned. He'll know how to value one who never changed.'

When he noted the sand in the glass and rose to take his

4

leave, he went out from the hall into the bright glitter of frost, and a vault of stars now three times larger than when first they appeared, and crackling with brilliance. The first real frost of the winter. As he made his way cautiously down the Wyle and out at the town gate he was thinking of the hard winter two years earlier, when the boy had been born, and hoping that this winter there would be no such mountainous snows and ferocious winds to drive it. This night, the eve of the Nativity, hung about the town utterly still and silent, not a breath to temper the bite of the frost. Even the movements of such men as were abroad seemed hushed and almost stealthy, afraid to shake the wonder.

No weather for boating with the River Severn all but frozen

5

The bridge had a sheen of silver upon it after the earlier fine rain. The river ran dark and still, with too strong a flow for frost to have any hold. A few voices gave him good night as he passed. In the rutted road of the Foregate he began to hurry, fearing he had lingered a little too long. The trees that sheltered the long riverside level of the Gaye loomed like the dark fur of the earth's winter pelt on his left hand, the flat, pale sheen of the mill-pond opened out on his right, beyond the six little abbey houses of grace, three on either side at the near end of the water, a narrow path slipping away from the road to serve each modest row. Silver and dark fell behind, he saw the torchlight glow from the gatehouse golden before him.

Still some twenty paces short of the gate he glimpsed a tall black figure sweeping towards him with long, rapid, fierce strides. The sidelong torchlight snatched it into momentary brightness as it strode past, the darkness took it again as it swept by Cadfael without pause or glance, long staff ringing against the frosty ruts, wide black garments flying, head and shoulders thrusting forward hungrily, long pale oval of face fixed and grim, and for one instant a vagrant light from the opened door of the nearest house by the pool plucked two crimson sparks of fire from the dark pits of the eyes.

Cadfael called a greeting that was neither heeded nor heard. Father Ailnoth swept by, engendering round him the only turbulence in the night's stillness, and was lost in the dark. Like an avenging fury, Cadfael thought later, like a scavenging raven swooping through the Foregate to hunt out little venial sins, and consign the sinners to damnation.

Dick Whittington's Probable Birthplace

FLETCHER MOSS

In Shropshire we believe that young Richard from the village of Whittington went off to London in the early 1360s and, displaying typical Shropshire characteristics of initiative and determination, overcame problems aplenty to become three times Lord Mayor of London – and a great Christmas favourite. Fletcher Moss, with tongue in cheek, wrote this account of Dick's adventures.

Any one who is fond of cats, or Lord Mayors or success in life, the marrying of a beautiful girl with lots of money, the making of a fortune and immortal fame, is probably interested in Dick Whittington, and would like to learn from whence he came. Several counties claim the honour of his birth. A parson has written a book about him, full of assertions without proofs, fit for those who have plenty of faith, but not for those who wish to get at the facts, and a knight has enlarged upon it. Let me tell the tale in its oldest form, and then judge what is likely.

Once upon a time, in London's famous city, where the streets were paved with gold (it is now almost five hundred and fifty years ago), there was a certain rich merchant known as Hugh Fitz Warren, who found a poor lad starving on his doorstep. He took him in, in charity, and told his cook to give him food and find him work. The lad was an orphan, a stranger in the city, and the cook bullied him. An old pamphlet has preserved his first order: 'Clean the spit and dripping pan, make the fire and wind the jack, or I'll break your head with the ladle and make you a football.' He was the scullion, servant of servants, but his master's daughter, Mistress Alice, asked him about his kindred and gave him old clothes.

A merchant who stayed all night gave him a penny for cleaning his shoes. With this, his first money, he bought a cat, for the garret in which he slept was swarming with rats. The tale of the buying of the cat sounds true. A woman who had a good mouser offered it to him for sixpence, and he bought it for a penny. It is like a woman to ask sixpence for what was worth a penny, and not unlike a merchant prince to buy for a penny what may have been worth sixpence. That cat proved to be a great success, and it is very probable that through a cat Dick won his young mistress's favour and his first rise to fortune. Still he was unhappy. The cook would neither quit nor die, and as all the world knows Dick ran away early on All Hallows' Day. But the immortal chimes recalled him. Who does not know what was said by the bells of Bow?

'Turn a-gain, Whit-ting-ton
Thrice Lord Mayor of Lon-don!'

He did turn again. His master was venturing a ship, as a merchant's foreign business was then called, and all his servants (as the custom also was) had to venture something with him. This ensured their prayers and good wishes, gave them a share in the business, and was cooperation centuries before cooperation was heard of. Dick was told he would have to venture something, but he fell on his knees, and begged them not to jeer at him, for he had nought but a cat.

'Just the thing we want,' said the captain of the ship; 'it will keep down the rats.' So Dick ventured his all, which was rather speculative, and the mice at the merchant's house breathed freely again.

The ship got wrecked, and the cat was taken to the Sultan of Gingerbeer, which was somewhere in Barbary, where she was worth her weight in gold in ridding the palace of the rats, and the Sultan sent Dick a casket of jewels for her. When the old merchant saw those jewels, and who they were for, according to the Bill of Lading, he nudged Alice, and said, 'Alice, my lass, thou must have these jewels by hook or by crook. Dick's a good lad and steady; he would take care of thee when I am gone. Thou hadst better wed him, jewels and all.'

Now, Alice was no chicken; she was much older than Dick to start with, but she knew how to humour her father, for she was wise and good, and as beautiful as the young ladies in the Sunday-school picture books. So the old man sent for 'Mr' Whittington, and when Dick came he fell on his knees again, as was the custom in those days for a man to do to his master, and Alice gave him the casket of jewels, telling him they were his in return for the cat, and he said she had better keep them. She said 'Oh no, I couldn't really,' and simpered and giggled till her father ordered the wedding, and each of them made Mr Whittington a partner.

Then he became a mercer and merchant adventurer, being introduced on 'Change at Chepe, where he proved a nailer, for he made heaps of money, and was chosen for the city council, where he made more by fitting up the army for the French war, which was meritorious in those days, though it would be desperately wicked now, all showing how much better we are than our fathers, and how much nearer to heaven.

Thrice Lord Mayor of London, as the bells had foretold, but in time a childless widower, this *flos mercatorum* wrote: 'A

prudent, wise, and devout man should make . . . dedys of mercy and pite, and especially provide for those miserable persons whom the penurye of poverty insulteth . . . and to whom the power of bodily labour is interdicted.' Then he built churches, almshouses, hospitals, and a prison, some of which, or the relics of them, remain unto this day, but his own tomb is said to have been rifled by the parson, who stole even the inner leaden coffin. The church and all were burnt in the great fire of London, but the undying fame of Dick Whittington grew brighter than ever through nursery songs and ballads for children.

How much of all this is true? I see no reason to doubt the truth of anything except a few details. Where Dick came from is the riddle I am trying to unravel, and it seems to me that all the attempts to prove him of knightly family were made after his death, since he never mentioned his father or mother or even his own age, as though he had known nothing whatever of his birth. Namesakes might claim kinship when the rich man was dead, but where would be the romance of the poor lad's rise? It was about this time that it was becoming usual for the common people to have a surname, and he, a stranger and orphan in London, would most probably be called after the place of his birth, or from whence he came. Therefore I believe he was from some place named Whittington, there being several places of that name. It is somewhere recorded that Roger de Hampton, the vicar of Ellesmere, had given the lad a recommendation to the Prior of St Bartholomew's, London. This should be good evidence, as Hampton and Ellesmere are both near to Whittington in Shropshire and Roger was vicar there (*c.* AD 1361) when Dick set out to seek his fortune. Here also is another striking fact. The lords of Whittington for many centuries had been, and were then, the Warins, Fitz Warins, or Fitz Warrens, the same name as Dick's master. It therefore seems to me almost certain

that Dick came from Whittington in Shropshire, that he may have been an illegitimate son of some of the castle folk, and that he tried his luck with a family connection rather than at St Bartholomew's Priory.

An Extraordinary Year

This extract comes from a medieval chronicle of Shrewsbury. It is known as the Taylor Manuscript because it was in that part of a Dr Taylor's library bequeathed by him to Shrewsbury School in 1766. The original document is still in the school library. Here it is printed as transcribed by Revd Leighton for the Shropshire Archaeological Society and it is followed by two extracts from Salopian Shreds and Patches *which go some way to clarify it. The year in question is 1573.*

This yeare the mynysters in the churches of Shrewsberye against X'ras dyd all were theire crosse capps and whyte syrplesys wch longe tyme befor dyd leave them of contrarie to the queenes iniunct'ons.

This yeare from the begyninge of November untill wthin xiiij dayes of Candlemas the seasoon was so pleasannt and fayre wthout frost or any snowe to specke of that there apeeryd leaves upon hathorn and ploomtresse before X'ras and the koocow was hard songe & also seene x days before X'ras,

also there was at newe yeares daye serten tenannts in Shropshyre presentyd theyre Landlords wth greene geese.

This yeare one Yevan ap Davyd alias Yeven wever of Franckvill in Shrewsberie beinge a man above lx yeares in the X'ras hollydayes goinge up a tree uppon his backesyde wth a ladder to plucke downe a pyeametts neast fell downe and broosyd hys braynes that he nev' spacke but dyed wthin an howre after the fall.

The Church in Salop, Christmas 1573

'Noel,' who asks for the elucidation of the extract from the Taylor Manuscript, relating to the use of 'crosse capps and

The make-believe world of the movies created this Christmas scene in front of the old hospital building in St Mary's Place, Shrewsbury in April 1984 during the filming of *A Christmas Carol* in the town

white surplesys' by the clergy of Shrewsbury, 1573, should refer to Owen and Blakeway's *History of Shrewsbury*, vol. I, p. 357. There he will find that in 1565, Queen Elizabeth issued certain injunctions or 'Advertisements' as they were termed, concerning the ceremonial of the Church. These injunctions, which I gather were equivalent to a modern 'Order in Council,' had apparently remained unheeded in Shrewsbury till, in October 1573, the Lord President of the Marches and the Bishop of Lichfield visited the town as special commissioners, to enforce their observance, which accordingly began at the Christmas following. The clergy of Shrewsbury, who were of the Puritan school, had probably been accustomed at all services to wear the Geneva gown, which is the authorized official habit of the Lutheran and Calvinist clergy of the Continent, and I think of the Scotch Presbyterian also. Restricted to the use of the preacher, it lingered in the English Church though without any authority but that of custom; and of late years, as we know, it has become comparatively rare.

I cannot say what 'crosse capps' were, but a friend refers me to a passage in Archbishop Parker's Life (Bk 2 No. 28) where the Archbishop forbids the clergy to wear hats, directing them to wear caps except on journeys. In former times men seldom uncovered their heads, even within doors, except in the presence of their superiors, and the clergy were accustomed to wear what were called 'priests' caps', which were skull-caps with a square cap called a biretta over them. As these were removed at the mention of the Saviour's name, they were for convenience sewn together, and out of this combination by degrees developed the familiar 'trencher' or 'college' cap of modern times. The square cap which was the form in use in the sixteenth century occurs frequently in effigies and portraits of Elizabethan divines.

A Green Christmas

From the beginning of November 1573, until within fourteen days of Candlemas 1574 the season was so warm, fair and pleasant, that leaves appeared upon hawthorns and plum trees before Christmas; and the cuckoo was heard to sing, and was also seen ten days before Christmas. On New Year's Day, certain tenants in Shropshire presented their landlords with green peas.*

*'Green geese' has been changed to 'green peas', however, a green goose is a young, grass-fed bird usually eaten at Michaelmas and not fattened on corn for Christmas. To have green geese for New Year the birds would have had to hatch in the autumn and been grass-fed through the winter.
If this was the case, the seasons must have been all out of kilter, so perhaps global warming is not a new problem after all!

Salopian Songs of Praise

GORDON ASHMAN

Music has always had an important part to play in our Christmas celebrations but it is only relatively recently that the now so familiar carols have become part of our Christmas

tradition. Here an acknowledged expert takes a look at the county's splendid musical tradition and explains about West Gallery music.

At Christmas-time, for nearly 150 years, the villages and small towns of Shropshire resounded to the noise of the parish quire. It is hard to imagine a sound further removed from modern, chorally-trained, surpliced singers accompanied by an organ, than the earthy sound of the village blacksmith or shoemaker leading the men, women and children, flutes and 'hotboys', bassoons and bass-viols which made up the 'quire,' a richly varied mixture of instrumentalists and singers.

We know little of village musical customs in England before the eighteenth century, but from about 1750 until within living memory, a vigorous form of psalm and hymn singing flourished. At the same time, English country dance music developed its own joyful style and sound. The instrumentalists who played for the village hop or the squire's birthday dance also led the singers in sacred music in the parish church – in joyous, sometimes locally composed anthems at Christmas as well as the everyday psalms and hymns. The dance music spilled over into the hymns; the part-songs and harmonies of the psalms enriched the secular music.

This splendid village musical tradition was to be found from Durham to Dorset, from Kent to Cumbria, and at the heart of the country, in Shropshire, it was as rich and as widespread as anywhere in the land. In almost every parish where records from these times survive, entries are to be found for 'The Singing Master – teaching Psalm-singing – £2 for the year', 'Strings for the Base-Viol, for the use of the church – 2s–0d' or 'Paid the singing girls 5s–0d each – £1–5–0.' The custom of singing in this way seems to have grown from a desire to improve the quality of worship, and especially

singing, in English churches in the early 1700s. Church authorities at this time frequently wrote of the dreadful quality of psalm-singing, if there was any singing at all. Bishops and archdeacons wrote to village vicars and rectors, urging them 'to improve the psalmody and psalm-singing'. Hymns, incidentally, were only introduced later.

In Shropshire, the first evidence of these attempts to improve the quality of singing in the village is often an entry in the churchwardens' accounts 'for the purchase of a pitch-pipe'. The pitch-pipe looked something like a wooden whistle or recorder, with a centre rod which could be moved in and out to produce different notes, rather like a Swanee whistle. It was used to produce the starting notes of the psalm for the different voices in the quire – bass, tenor, counter-tenor or alto, and treble or soprano. A typical psalm (and one which is still heard today) might have been 'Old Hundredth' – 'All people that on earth do dwell'.

While pitch-pipes helped to improve the quality of the start of the psalms, the unaccompanied singers seem to have had trouble holding the rest of the tune. All too often we learn of 'dreadful discord in the quire this morning' in diary entries of these times. Two steps were taken to correct such discords in many Shropshire parishes: the purchase of musical instruments to help the singers hold the tune, and the engagement of singing masters to teach singing and the rudiments of music.

The earliest purchases of instruments were often made to help the bass line – bassoons, bass-viols or violoncellos; 'hotboys' or 'hobys' (from the French word hautbois, the high wood or oboe) were added later; clarinets and flutes came along; few churches bought violins or fiddles, but they often paid for strings for such instruments, suggesting that the players owned the instruments but the parish paid for the strings. At about this time, between 1750 and 1800, many

Shropshire parish records begin to show payments to psalm-singing masters, many of whom had Welsh-sounding names such as Owens, Jones, and Davies. One of their number, Edward Edwards, nearly bankrupted Oswestry in 1783 when he was engaged 'to Instruct the Inhabitants in Psalm-Singing . . . and be paid ten shillings and sixpence each time he attends.' He attended so often that he sent the parish a bill for £41–10–0 and a special rate had to be raised to pay him off.

As interest in this music grew, so quires became larger, and finding a place for the quire in the church became a problem. Most pews were owned by individuals, or the right to use them went with the ownership of a particular property in the parish – thus there was nowhere for a large group of singers and instrumentalists to sit or perform. Most Shropshire churches lie east to west, with the chancel and altar at the east end, but a little space was to be found at the west end. The answer to the problem was to erect a gallery for the quire on wooden or cast-iron posts. Not many of these galleries survived late-Victorian 'restoration' but lovely examples can be seen at Stokesay or Petton, which also has fine old box pews.

The work of the singing teachers, some of whom were also composers, together with the use of instruments and the growing musical knowledge of the quire members led to the high point of what is now called West Gallery music between 1800 and 1850. Until this time, many vicars would allow nothing but psalms to be sung in their churches, since only the holy words of the bible were permitted for worship. However, the growing influence of men like John Wesley and George Whitefield, and Wesley's brother Charles, who alone wrote between 6,000 and 9,000 hymns, forced the established church to accept such 'frivolities'. Wonderful, ringing tunes were written for the hymns, anthems were composed at Adderley and Bishop's Castle, churchwardens paid for candles

so that the village quires could rehearse their Christmas offerings in the galleries on dark November evenings, adult singers were rewarded with beer or cider, the singing girls paid with 'ribbands'. The quires from hamlets such as Roddington and Uppington competed to outdo each other at singing nights, blacksmiths practised on the clarionet, carpenters on the cello, masons played flutes, farmers the bassoon, and the retired soldier who had learnt to play in a military band wrestled with the serpent – eight feet of leather-bound walnut, shaped like a gigantic snake. A serpent may be seen in Clive House Museum in Shrewsbury.

The successes of the village quires eventually brought about their undoing. Led by sturdy tradesmen, yeoman farmers, or independent artisans, they became a powerful force in village life. No secular function was complete without their music; no sacred event was complete without their sound, and this situation inevitably led to conflict with the vicars who felt that the quires often 'got above themselves'. Rectors are known to have left the church the moment the quire started to perform. In retaliation, quires obtained curtains for the galleries, which they noisily closed the moment the vicar began his sermon, often loudly tuning-up their instruments when they thought a sermon had gone on too long. Battles between clergy and quire were often bitter and sometimes long-lasting, but eventually, the clerics won. Quires were replaced by choirs – conformable little boys in surplices who did as they were told, and barrel organs and harmoniums (played by the vicars' daughters) replaced the instruments of the village bands. Many Church of England quires responded to this by simply crossing the road to the Methodist chapels, where they continued to play such music until the present century, but for the most part the tradition withered and died.

However, let us return to Shropshire at Christmastide in the heyday of West Gallery music. Most quires obtained

Church and cottage at Market Drayton

copies of the music they used by buying one printed copy of a psalm or hymn book which was usually kept in the parish chest. Each musician or singer then copied out their particular part into their own music book, and the quire leader copied out the score. In Shropshire villages we might have found the quires preparing their Christmas offerings from the books of the Wesleys or Isaac Watts, Dr Dodderidge and Thomas Clark. In some cases, the village musicians composed their own tunes to celebrate the birth of the Lord, but in many cases, they borrowed or adapted tunes to go with the words 'While shepherds watched their flocks by night'. This was one of the best-loved Christmas hymns, and was permitted from the earliest days of the quires, since the text was from chapter two of St Luke's gospel. Today, we all sing 'While shepherds' to the tune Winchester Old, but this tune and these words were rarely heard together until they were published in *Hymns, Ancient and Modern*, in 1861. Before that time each village simply used its own favourite tune. There are at least fifteen different tunes to be found in Shropshire collections which would have fitted the words.

Finally, in parishes on Shropshire's border with Wales, in places such as Llanyblodwel, the custom of Christmas carolling survived. The old tradition of the village quire going round the houses of the village and the outlying farms in the bitter cold of a Christmas night, singing, in the words of the old documents, until 'plygain' (or in English, until dawn), led by a harper, and warmed by drinks paid for by the churchwardens continued well into the nineteenth century, although the churchwardens ceased to pay for the custom after 1827.

A Christmas tune with strong Shropshire connections was Jerusalem, sometimes called Comfort. This is not the Jerusalem of the Women's Institute – 'And did those feet, in

ancient times, walk upon England's pasture green' – but a lovely tune now linked with Isaac Watts' words 'Joy to the World'. The words are to be found in a number of hymn books used throughout the county and the best example of the tune comes from the manuscript book of John Moore, a young nurseryman from Wellington, which is dated 1837–1839. When the clergy banned the old quires from the churches and replaced them with barrel-organs, they were still forced to use the parishioners' favourite tunes. In 1839, Albrighton (near Shifnal) asked the London makers of their barrel-organ to include the tune Comfort, but they replied 'Comfort we do not know by that name'.

It has been suggested that the tune was taken from Handel; he was certainly fond of using these four, falling opening notes, and village composers borrowed heavily from his music, but the true composer remains unknown. However, the writer of the words, Dr Isaac Watts (1674–1748), was both known and inspired. His best-known hymn – 'When I survey the wondrous cross' remains popular today.

If a modern choir wishes to try to reproduce the sound made by a quire, they should have their sopranos or trebles sing the top line at pitch, helped by a flute; the second line is for altos and counter-tenors, helped by a fiddle; the line marked 'Air' should be sung an octave below the written line by tenors, helped by one or two sopranos and a clarinet at pitch; the basses should sing the bottom line, helped by a cello or bassoon.

JOY TO THE WORLD

1. *f*   Joy to the World! the Lord is come;
        Let earth receive her King;
        Let every heart prepare him room,
        And heav'n and nature sing.

2. *f* Joy to the earth! the Saviour reigns;
         Let men their songs employ;
         While fields and floods, rocks, hills and plains,
         Repeat the sounding joy.

3. *p* No more let sins and sorrows grow,
         Nor thorns infest the ground;
    cr He comes to make the blessings flow
         Far as the curse is found.

4. *f* He rules the world with truth and grace,
         And makes the nations prove
         The glories of his righteousness,
         And wonders of his love.

Jerusalem or Comfort   C. M.

Joy to the world! the Lord is come; Let earth re-ceive her King. Let ev-ery heart pre-pare Him

air

Joy to the world! the Lord is come; Let earth receive her King. Let ev-ery heart pre-pare Him

room, and heav'n and nature sing, and heav'n and na-ture sing, and heav'n, and heav'n and na-ture sing.

room, and heav'n and nature sing, and heav'n and nature sing, and heav'n, and heav'n and na-ture sing.

The Victorian Visitor

BERYL COPSEY

A young American girl spent Christmas at Ludlow in 1851 and had a very happy time as this piece, which is based on her letters, explains.

Does it get right to your romantic heart, that candlelit Victorian dinner-table scene of a million Christmas cards? Papa all whiskered and cheery, carving knife poised to attack a turkey almost as bulbous as himself while Mama in a lace cap sits serenely beaming at a brood of oh-so-cherubic children. Aaaah! But have you ever wondered what they would do when that tableau broke up, or how their celebration had been organized anyway?

We might look for such information at the festive doings, in December 1851, of a household near Ludlow, events which were faithfully recorded by the letters of their rather unusual visitor. For who would have expected to find a real-life, Gone-with-the-Wind type of Southern belle in that small English country town? Miss Anna Maria Fay, of Savannah in Georgia, had landed in Liverpool during the autumn, paused there long enough to buy herself an umbrella, and had then taken the new-fangled railway train for Shrewsbury before riding down to Ludlow by stagecoach to complete her long journey.

As a young lady of merely 23 years she had naturally, in those years of Victorian propriety, to be accompanied by a chaperone aunt, their intention being to spend almost a year with other relatives then living at The Moor.

By the end of November Anna Maria had settled happily into her unfamiliar surroundings. She was quite resigned to the cold climate and had quickly resolved the problem (most odd to her way of thinking), of the female fashion which called for a high-collared day dress to be replaced by a low-cut evening toilette at dinner time.

'Imagine walking through a great hall, sitting in a cold dining-room with nothing over my neck,' she wrote to her mother, adding the reassurance that she had had her silk shawl lined with warm tweed so that all was now well. An ingenious solution, don't you think – though perhaps somewhat bulky?

Miss Anna had also managed to convince neighbouring families that she was neither an uncivilized savage nor did she speak in some outlandish Red Indian gibberish. On the other hand she had learned that to comment on the state of the weather was an essential part of conversation whilst in England. In time, too, her singing of the negro spiritual songs of her homeland became the high-spot of local after-dinner entertainment.

Anna Maria's letter of 16 December told, with excitement, 'Christmas is to be celebrated in true English style'. And certainly plans were beginning to take shape. Though four cousins had provided her with youthful company since her arrival, there was now added their most presentable elder brother down from Oxford and he had brought with him a friend, 'full of fun and humour, just the sort of person to enter into a frolic'. So the scene was set and the cast assembled.

Two days before THE day was then considered sufficient time for the final preparations, when the young men

Snow on the roads in Ironbridge still causes motorists to think twice
before tackling challenges like Jigger's Bank

cheerfully offered to climb the highest trees in search of mistletoe. That notion was soon vetoed by Uncle Richard, who 'dampened their ardour by ordering the gardener to perform the important duty' of collecting the mistletoe boughs.

Next, with much whispering in corners, it became clear that a splendid charade was to be shown. It was to be quite an event, not at all the extempore party game we know today, but an organized and well-rehearsed playlet.

And alas, poor Anna Maria would only be able to watch the performance for, as an unmarried girl, it was just 'not done' that she should take to the stage, even on such a family occasion. Instead, any part for a female would be played by Aunt Catherine, the safely mature mother of five.

At last it was Christmas Eve, and with it came carols – 'some boys chanted outside the windows the story of the Saviour's birth, the church bells rang and all told of the coming day'. Anna Maria, born in the New World, prepared enthusiastically to share in the traditions of an Old World Christmas.

So it was, when everyone retired to bed the resident ghost – oh yes, like all old houses this one had seen tragedy – might have heard much rustling of paper, noticed much peeping from partly opened doors and been amazed as one occupant after another tiptoed furtively about the corridors. In fact, a stocking hung on the handle of each bedroom door, there to receive gifts for the one within. So, 'what with running from door to door and then listening at our own until our stocking were filled we did not get to bed until one o'clock'. No wonder then, 'I must confess we overslept on Christmas morning'.

Awakening, Anna Maria found herself the recipient of bracelets, brooches, books and chocolates before going down to breakfast where 'each has something pretty to show, and

"Merry Christmas" passes from mouth to mouth. Everyone is happy, everyone joyful.'

Then, at last, the baskets full of holly and mistletoe were brought in to decorate the house and while the children painted little English and American flags to string along the mantlepiece, Anna Maria set off on horseback to pull sheep's wool from the hedges for a wig required by the charade.

At the then-fashionable hour of five the whole family sat down to dine, with the four excited children promoted from their nursery meal for the occasion. 'We ate English dishes,' explained a letter home to America, which makes it a pity that the centrepiece was 'boiled turkey', sounding far from festive. However, there was plum pudding to follow and the meal must have included fruit from those hothouses which were the pride of every Victorian estate owner; 'grapes, apricots, figs and peaches' had already figured in Miss Anna's reports of the Ludlow lifestyle. And to drink, surely there must have been something a little extra to the ordinary 'I drink every day at lunch a glass of port and at dinner a large goblet of ale.'

After dinner The Moor began to fill with neighbouring families, invited to swell the numbers for a few dances – when there was much male skirmishing to position partners beneath the mistletoe – and then to watch the charade, obviously intended as the climax of the festive evening.

The absurd breach-of-promise case which was acted out to indicate the first syllable caused Anna Maria to laugh so much that she had doubts about the holding power of the hooks on her bodice. Next came a nautical scene which led everyone to guess that 'ship' was the term being illustrated, and though by now they all knew that the complete word must be 'courtship' they would not excuse the actors from finishing the play.

So we hear of an interesting interpretation, considering that 1851 was still pre-suffragist time. For Aunt Catherine

Bringing in the Christmas pudding

appeared in long pantalettes and a short dress as Miss Fanny Bloomer and proceeded to harass a shy young man with her ardour. Now that Society no longer expected a woman to hide her love, cried Miss Fanny, she availed herself of her sex's new privileges and offered him her hand and her heart. Needless to say the young man was rescued in the nick of time, and to much applause.

'It was admirably acted,' was Anna Maria's only, and rather subdued, comment – which leaves us wondering if she ever longed to use such a freedom? We can never know, but must remember that she returned home at the end of her holiday to live out the long years of her life as the Fay family's favourite maiden aunt.

That Victorian evening of Christmas Day was rounded off with more dancing before the visitors departed, leaving their hosts to fulfil another fine old English tradition, to draw chairs round the fireside and tell ghost stories by the light of its flickering flames.

The Moor had its own sad tale of murder and haunting, the

fateful triangle of a beautiful girl, one chosen suitor and one rejected one, this last her own cousin, the son and heir to the house. A situation leading to double murder and a suicide.

'There was a fascination about it from which you cannot get away,' was Anna Maria's verdict, apparently quite unperturbed by the fact that she occupied the bedroom in which that earlier girl had been stabbed to death.

A few days later that particular Christmas account ended in a way only too familiar to most of us still. 'December 29th. Everything is too tight for me, the insertion on my white muslin burst asunder down the entire length and the seam down one side gave way.' Luckily there was to be, for Anna Maria, a trip to London during which she replenished her wardrobe for the further months of her English holiday.

from

The Diaries of Hannah Cullwick

Hannah Cullwick was born in Shifnal and worked most of her life as a servant, sometimes in Shropshire but also in London and other parts of the country. In 1854 she met Arthur Munby, an upper-class author and poet with an obsessive interest in working women. The couple eventually married but theirs was always a very strange relationship. Hannah acted

the part of Munby's servant – almost slave – and yet it was Hannah who set the boundaries of the relationship. She would not play the part of a 'lady' and for many years refused to give up work.

At Munby's request she kept a diary so that he could learn the minute detail of her daily life. The diaries reveal the hard work that went on below stairs to ensure a comfortable life for those who lived up stairs. At Christmas in 1863 Hannah was working in Kilburn for the Foster family. Hannah returned to live in Shropshire in 1877. She no longer kept a diary but we know that she lived in the county, or briefly with relatives in Staffordshire, until her death in 1909.

Although her husband did not live with her, he did visit regularly until she died at the age of seventy-six. Munby died the following year, aged eighty, and his will, which finally revealed their secret life and love, made headlines in the national press in July 1910.

Wednesday 23 December (1863)

I got up early and lighted the kitchen fire to get it up soon for the roasting – a turkey and eight fowls for tomorrow, being Christmas Eve, and forty people's expected and they're going to have a sort o' play. And so they are coming tonight to do it over and the Missis has order'd a hot supper for 15 people. Very busy indeed all day and worried too with the breakfast and the bells ringing so and such a deal to think about as well as work to do. I clean'd 2 pairs o' boots and the knives. Wash'd the breakfast things up. Clean'd the passage and shook the door mat. Got the dinner and clean'd away after, keeping the fire well up and minding the things what was roasting and basting 'em till I was nearly sick wi' the heat and smell. The waiter came at 5 o'clock, I made the coffee and

Hannah Cullwick: upstairs

that and give the waiter it as he come for it up to 7 o'clock. Fred Crook came in and help'd me and I was glad of him as well as for company. We got the supper by a quarter to ten, and we run up and downstairs to see some of the acting – just in the passage, and saw 'em all in their kings' and queens' dresses. The queen of Spain was Miss Head and she come and spoke to me and I answer'd her, 'Madam' and she laugh'd. We laid the kitchen cloth and had our supper and clean'd away after. I took the ham and pudding up at 12 o'clock, made the fire up and put another on and then to bed. Came down again at 4 for the waits woke me just in time. The fire wanted stirring and more coals on and when I'd got the pudding boiling again I went to bed till after six. Got up and dress'd myself then and clean'd the tables and hearth and got the kettle boiling and so began.

Thursday 24 December

After breakfast I clean'd a pair o' boots and lighted the fires upstairs. Swept and dusted the room and the hall. Laid the cloth for breakfast and took it up when the bell rang. Put the beef down to roast. Clean'd the knives. Made the custards and mince pies – got the dinner up. Clean'd away after and wash'd up in the scullery. Clean'd the kitchen tables and hearth. Made the fire up again and fill'd the kettle. Made the coffee, wash'd myself a bit and put a clean apron on and give the waiters the coffee and milk as they ask'd for it. Fred Crook came in again and help'd me with the dishes and knives. We had supper in the kitchen and then I dish'd up for the parlour. Lots o' sweets came from Carter's and the jellies and the man dish'd 'em up. We went upstairs and stood in the dining-room door case and saw the acting in the other room. Mr Saunderson the cardinal came and spoke to us servants and was going to shake hands but I said, 'My hands are dirty, sir'. There was four singers the Master got in for the night, so I

Hannah Cullwick: downstairs

ran up and listen'd to 'em and they sang capitally I think. After supper was over the Master had the hot mince pie up wi' a ring and sixpence in it – they had good fun over it, 'cause Mr Grant got the ring and a young lady sixpence. We had no fun downstairs, all was very busy till 4 o'clock and then to bed.

Christmas Day Friday 25 December

Got up at eight and lit the fires. Took the drugget up and shook it and laid it down again in the dining room. Rubb'd the furniture and put straight. Had my breakfast. Clean'd a pair o' boots. Wash'd the breakfast things up and the dishes. Clean'd the front steps. Took the breakfast upstairs. Got the dinner and fill'd the scuttles. The family went up the Hill for the evening and I clean'd myself to go and see Ellen, but I'd such a headache and felt *so* tired and sleepy I sat in a chair and slept till five and then had tea and I felt better. It was a beautiful moonlight night and I walk'd up to the Grove and sat with them thern [*sic*] servants. Had a little supper and home again to bed at ten.

Saturday 26 December

I lighted the fires and black'd the grates – the kitchen grate was so greasy I'd to wash it over first. I felt glad the Christmas was over so far for if it kept on long as it's bin the last 3 or 4 days I should be knock'd up I think. I clean'd 2 pairs o' boots. Swept and dusted the room and the hall and got the breakfast up. The Missis came down into the kitchen and look'd round at what was left, and paid me my quarter's wages. She saw I'd got a mistletoe hanging up and I told her ther'd bin no one kiss'd yet. She gave me the money for the Christmas boxes to the men and boys same as last year and I give 'em as they came. I got a lot too – near two lbs [£2] in all. They was sent to me – Mr Grant 3s 4d and Mr Saunderson

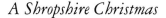

the same, Mr Hous 5*s* and old Mrs Foster 2*s* 6*d*, the rest was from the tradespeople. I put mine in the bank wi' my wages – Mary says hers shall buy a new bonnet. I clean'd the kitchen and the passage and the stairs and wash'd up in the scullery. Got the supper over and to bed at ten.

from

A Night in the Snow

REVD DONALD CARR

The Long Mynd is a high moorland area reaching some 1,700 ft above sea level in the south west of the county. Those who visit the area only in summer may consider it rather exposed, yet beautiful and benign. Those who live there have more respect. In a severe winter these hills are treacherous for the unwary – as the Revd Donald Carr discovered one Sunday in 1865.

This gentleman ministered to two parishes: his base at Woolstaston as well as the church at Ratlinghope. Some four miles of mountain track across the highest part of the Long Mynd separates the two churches. For many years, in spite of snow, fog, gales and rain, the Revd Carr had always managed to hold services in both parishes every Sunday. So on

*29 January 1865 he saw no reason why he should not set out
for Ratlinghope after morning service at Woolstaston, even
though it was already snowing heavily. He reached the church,
held a service for the few parishioners who had turned up,
refused all offers of hospitality for the night and started back to
Woolstaston, intending to hold a 6 p.m. service there.*

The extracts that follow are from A Night in the Snow, *the
Revd Carr's understated account of his struggle to survive the
arctic-like conditions on the return journey.*

After a while I became aware that the ground under my feet
was the wrong shape, sloping downwards when it should
have been level and I then knew that I had missed my way.
This, however, gave me no great uneasiness, as I imagined
that I had only gone a little too much to the south of the
wood, and that I should soon reach an inhabited district at
the bottom of it, known as Bullock's Moor, from which a
somewhat circuitous route would bring me safely home.
Under this impression I walked cheerfully on, but only for a
few steps further. Suddenly my feet flew from under me,
and I found myself shooting at a fearful pace down the side
of one of the steep ravines which I had imagined lay further
away to my right. I thought to check myself by putting my
stick behind me, and bearing heavily upon it in the manner
usual under such circumstances in alpine travelling. Before,
however, I could do so I came in contact with something
which jerked it out of my hand and turned me round, so
that I continued my tremendous glissade head downwards,
lying on my back.

I never lost consciousness, but had time to think much of
those I should leave behind me, expecting every moment as I
did to be dashed over the rocks at the bottom of the ravine;
knew in fact that such must be my fate, unless I could stop

The Lawley, near Church Stretton, dusted with snow

myself by some means. Owing to the softness of the snow, I contrived to accomplish this by kicking my foot as deep into the snow as I could, and at the same time bending my knee with a smart muscular effort, so as to make a hook of my leg; this brought me to a standstill, but my position was anything but agreeable even then, hanging head downwards on a very steep part, and never knowing any moment but that I might start again.

With much difficulty, however, I at length succeeded in getting myself the right way up, and then descended with great care to the bottom of the ravine, intending if possible to walk along the course of the stream in its hollow till it should lead me to the enclosed country. The ravine, however, was so

choked up with snow, that to walk along the valley was utterly impossible. The drifts were many feet over my head, in several places they must have been at least 20 ft in depth; and having once got into them, I had the greatest difficulty, by scratching and struggling, to extricate myself from them again. It was now dark. I did not know into which of the ravines I had fallen, for at this part there is a complete network of them intersecting each other in every direction. The only way by which I had thought to escape was hopelessly blocked up, and I had to face the awful fact that I was lost among the hills, should have to spend the night there, and that, humanly speaking, it was almost impossible that I could survive it.

I only ventured to take my brandy very sparingly, wishing to husband it as much as possible, and there was but a very tiny drop left. My hands were so numbed with cold as to be nearly useless. I had the greatest difficulty in holding the flask, or in eating snow for refreshment, and could hardly get my hands to my mouth for the masses of ice which had formed upon my whiskers, and which were gradually developing into a long crystal beard, hanging halfway to my waist. Icicles likewise had formed about my eyes and eyebrows, which I frequently had to break off, and my hair had frozen into a solid block of ice. After the loss of my hat, my hair must, I suppose, have become filled with snow, while I was overhead in the drifts. Probably this was partially melted by the warmth of my head, and subsequently converted into ice by the intense frost. Large balls of ice also formed upon my cuffs and underneath my knees, which encumbered me very much in walking, and I had continually to break them off.

Never did a shipwrecked mariner watch for the morning more anxiously than did I through that weary, endless night, for I knew that a glimpse of the distance in any one direction

would enable me to steer my course homewards. Day dawned at last, but hope and patience were to be yet further tried, for a dense fog clung to the face of the hill, obscuring everything but the objects close at hand. Furthermore I discovered I was rapidly becoming snow blind. My eyes which had been considerably injured already by the sharp sleet of the evening before, were further affected by the glare of the snow, and I was fast losing all distinctness of vision. Owing to my failing eyesight, my falls became very frequent, and several of them were from heights so great that it would scarcely be believed were I to attempt to describe them.

My method of progression was more crawling than walking, as I had to drive my hands deep into the snow, and clutch at tufts of grass or heather, or anything I could find beneath it to hold on by. I must have gone forward in this way for an hour or two, when I found the ravine becoming less steep, and I heard the sound of running water very distinctly. Accordingly I thought I would descend and try once more whether I could walk down the stream, as this by its sound seemed a larger one, and I thought it might have cut a way through the drifts. I reached the bottom of the valley safely – it appears to have been the valley immediately above the Light Spout waterfall – and trying to walk by the stream, I tumbled over the first upper fall. Hearing a noise of falling water and seeing dimly rocks all around me, I found it would not do to go forward in this direction, so, having unconsciously gone to the very edge of the lower cascade, where I must in all probability have been killed had I fallen over, I turned sharply up the hill again, going over the rocks above, and coming down again by a very steep place.

But a new misfortune now befell me: I lost my boots. They were strong laced boots, without elastic sides, or any such weak points about them. I had observed before that one was

getting loose, but was unable to do anything about it, from the numbness of my hands; and after struggling out of a deep drift prior to re-ascending the hill, I found that I had left this boot behind. There was nothing for it but to go on without, and as my feet were perfectly numbed from the cold, and devoid of feeling, I did not experience any difficulty or pain on this account. That boot was afterwards found on a ledge of rock near the waterfall. I soon after lost the other one, or rather, I should say, it came off, and I could not get it on again, so I carried it in my hand some time, but lost it in one of my many severe falls.

And so for hours I walked on in my stockings without inconvenience. Even when I trod upon gorse bushes, I did not feel it as my feet had become as insensible as my hands. It had occurred to me now that I might be in the Carding Mill valley, and that I would steer my course on that supposition. It was fortunate that I did so, for I was beginning to think that I could not hold out much longer, and was struggling in a part where drifts were up nearly to my neck, when I heard what I thought never to hear again – the blessed sound of human voices. Children's voices, talking and laughing, and apparently sliding not very far off. I called to them with all my might, but judge to my dismay when sudden and total silence took the place of the merry voices I had so lately heard! I shouted again and again, and said that I was lost, but there was no reply.

It appeared, as I learned afterwards, that these children saw me, though I could not see them, and ran away terrified at my unearthly aspect. Doubtless the head of a man protruding from a deep snow drift, crowned and bearded with ice like a ghastly emblem of winter, was a sight to cause a panic among children, and one cannot wonder that they ran off to communicate the news that 'there was a bogie in the snow'.

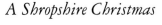

Happily, however, for the bogie, he had noticed the direction from which these voices came, and struggling forward again, I soon found myself sufficiently near to the Carding Mill to recognize the place, blind as I was. A little girl now ventured to approach me as, true to the instincts of her nature, the idea dawned upon her that I was no goblin of the mountains, no disagreeable thing from a world beneath popped up through the snow, but a real fellow-creature in distress. I spoke to her and told her that I was the clergyman of Ratlinghope, and had been lost in the snow on the hill all night. As she did not answer at once, I suppose she was taking a careful observation of me, for after a few moments she said, 'Why, you look like Mr Carr of Woolstaston'. 'I am Mr Carr,' I replied; whereupon the boys who had previously run away, and as I imagine, taken refuge behind the girl, came forward and helped me on to the little hamlet, only a few yards distant, where some half dozen cottages are clustered together round the Carding Mill.

After 27 hours in freezing conditions, Revd Carr finally reached home, where all hope of his safe return had long since been given up. He suffered no permanent damage as a result of his adventure and lived on until 1900, convinced he had been saved by God's help and his own refusal to sleep or even rest throughout his long ordeal.

from

Shropshire Folk-lore

CHARLOTTE BURNE

Charlotte Burne was born in Staffordshire in 1850, but it was the folk-lore of Shropshire which became her great passion and main interest. In 1883 she completed a book called Shropshire Folk-lore *which is still an important reference work for anyone interested in the county's traditions and superstitions. This extract is from the chapter on Christmas.*

Few will need to be told that the Christmas season consists of twelve days besides Christmas Day, which are commonly spoken of in Shropshire as one period, 'the Christmas'. Such a thing happened, the folk say, 'in the Christmas', 'before Christmas was out', or 'between the two Christmases', i.e. between Christmas Day and Old Christmas Day, which falls on our present Twelfth Day.

Preparation for Christmas, besides killing of beasts and poultry, compounding of mincemeat and mixing of puddings, included a great and general house-cleaning. A maid must be slovenly indeed who would permit anything under her care to remain dirty at Christmas. In West Shropshire, in olden days (in the early years of the century), industrious maids would set

themselves tasks, so many 'slippings of yarn' or other achievements, to be completed before the 'Christmas cleaning' began. Then the labourers' wives were called in to help and everything was scrubbed to the utmost pitch of cleanliness. The pewter and brazen vessels had to be made so bright that the maids could see to put their caps on in them – otherwise the fairies woud pinch them; but if all was perfect, the worker would find a coin in her shoe; which famous old English belief, we are told, was much encouraged by their mistresses, who would sometimes slip the expected reward into its place themselves, to excite their servants to industry.

One special care was putting away any suds or 'buck-lee' for washing purposes, both of which it was most unlucky to keep in the house during 'the Christmas'. They were therefore poured away on Christmas Eve, and all the empty household vessels were carefully left clean and dry. Some also 'put away leaven out of their houses'.

Then the clean cheerful family kitchen must be adorned with holly and ivy. Sprigs of bright-berried holly, alternating with the darker ivy, are stuck in the small leaden panes of the window casements, among the willow-pattern plates and dishes on the dark oak 'dresser', and the tall brass candlesticks, 'chaney ornaments', and 'crock dogs' on the high mantelshelf. Nowadays, a bunch of evergreen, with a piece of mistletoe dependent from it, is hung from the middle of the ceiling, or sometimes in the doorway, at the same time, but 'by rights', old-fashioned people say (and I know some who still observe the practice,) the 'kissing bush' should not be hung up till New Year's Eve, in readiness for the romp which replaced the primitive fashion of New Year's greetings. The New Year's mistletoe should be carefully preserved till it is superseded by a new piece at the next New Year, but the Christmas talismans of holly and ivy are always removed at the end of the winter season.

Half a century ago, the scene of lighting the hearth-fire on Christmas Eve, to continue burning throughout the Christmas season, might have been witnessed in the hill-country of West Shropshire, from Chirbury and Worthen to Pulverbatch and Pontesbury. . . .

There are many yet living in this retired and beautiful district who can remember seeing the 'Christmas Brand', a great trunk of seasoned oak, holly, yew or crab-tree, drawn by horses to the farmhouse door, and thence, with the aid of rollers and levers, placed at the back of the wide open hearth, where the fire was made up in front of it. . . .

Mr Thomas Powell tells us that he has often seen the log drawn in by men with a rope, and that about 1860, he witnessed the scene of bringing in the log at an old farmhouse in Corve Dale, where the farm servants cooked and ate their meals in a great room, a brew-house or back-kitchen, with a flagged floor, and no grate, but a stone hearth raised about four inches above the floor, where burnt a wood fire fed with logs four or five feet long, which lay with one end resting on a brick or stone. On Christmas Eve the waggoner brought into this primitive abode an enormous log which was drawn to the hearth by a horse, and kept burning until it was entirely consumed, which was not till nearly dawn on the second morning. The servants sat up in the great open chimney watching it, and continually raking the sticks up to it, so as to keep the fire alive till the last possible moment, and 'there was great fun among the lads and lasses vying with each other "who should see the Clerk go out"', namely, the last spark fly up the chimney after all the 'congregation' had been dismissed.

I have not yet met with instances of the observances of these customs elsewhere in the country, but they must once have prevailed more generally. The Gentleman's Magazine for 1790 relates the reminiscences of an old lady to the effect

A Shropshire scene ideal for any Christmas card

that during the Civil Wars, Haughmond Abbey, then the dwelling-house of the Barker family, was set on fire by the yule-log. And to this day the curfew bell at Cleobury Mortimer is silent during 'the Christmas', showing that then the fires might not be extinguished.

Everywhere we hear of the need that each household should be able to keep up its own hearth-fire during Christmas. 'Permit me to say,' writes an aged and often-quoted correspondent of *Salopian Shreds and Patches*, 'that I well remember, some threescore and ten Christmas days ago, residing in one of two isolated dwellings at Hanwood (near Shrewsbury), no other house being within a quarter of a mile. We were very good neighbours, willing to help each other in time of need; but there was one time of need when neither neighbour dared to approach the other. Asking to borrow a

bit of fire, or even to ask for a light to a candle, on Christmas Day or any day until after Old Twelfth Day, was the greatest insult we could offer to a neighbour, as nothing was so certain to cause bad luck to a family for the ensuing year, as to fetch fire (from their house) during Christmas-time. Consequently it was no trifling undertaking on Christmas Eve to arrange the tinder-box with all its implements in the art of striking a light: first to obtain a large piece of old linen rag, and well burn it into tinder; and then the flint and steel to be looked up and cleaned, or new ones bought in Shrewsbury market; next, the match-making – generally small bits of brown paper cut to sharp points at one end, then the brimstone melted in an old iron spoon, into which the bits of paper were dipped; and all carefully laid by in a dry place until Christmas morning. If each family attended to these precautions carefully, then we should be sure to be good neighbours all the year round.'

The Curmudgeons' Christmas

RANDOLPH CALDECOTT

Randolph Caldecott (1846–86) was probably the most popular illustrator of his time. Born in Cheshire, his first job was as a bank clerk in Whitchurch and later he used this north Shropshire town as the backcloth for many of his carefully

*observed and very detailed drawings. His days as a bank clerk
were soon over once he established himself as a talented
illustrator, with regular commissions from publications such as
this one in December 1885 for* The Graphic.

One young and two elderly curmudgeons, strangers to each
other, all travelling on Christmas Eve to evade the seasonable
festivities of their respective relatives, are obliged to put up at
a farm-house inn: one of them because his horse is lame, the
others because of an accident to a coach. The landlord assures
them that he will make them quite comfortable. The
travellers are grumpy towards each other, especially when they
find that they must all dine together at the same table. Each
takes his pint of wine, and wonders at the little lady of some
six or seven years who dines too.

The child has pretty and engaging ways, and after dinner
she inveigles the three gentlemen into playing at 'Puss in the
Corner', calling in the landlord's daughter to make up the

'The travellers are grumpy . . . especially when they find that they
must all dine together'

47

required number. About noon on Christmas Day a Mr Rosey and his three daughters, on their way to a country house further on, arrive at the inn. Their own horses are done up by reason of the snow, and they can get no relays. So they agree to stay and dine at the host's table. An excellent dinner is served, and the grim faces of the old curmudgeons somewhat relax at sight of the turkey and the chine; while the arrival of the plum-pudding and a glance from the eldest Miss Rosey cause the youngest curmudgeon – whose name is Wildboy – almost to thaw, but not quite. At dessert-time arrive three young gentlemen, who have previous acquaintance with the Roseys, and who have been sent by the neighbouring squire to seek them. The landlord is begged by Mr Rosey to 'fill the flowing bowl until it does run over', and it is emptied in honour of various toasts, but somehow not to the enjoyment of Mr Wildboy. Word is then given to clear the kitchen. 'Turn the Trencher' is played by request of the little girl, Mr W.

'Next they have a "country dance"'

having to pay forfeits under the mistletoe bush. Next they have a 'country dance', some of the gentlemen appearing in shoes borrowed from the jovial host. One of them is unluckily forced to keep behind the settle, having strained his pantaloons during his efforts at 'Turn the Trencher'.

Afterwards they play at 'Blindman's Buff' to the great delight of the younger part of the company. The evening closes with another scene under the mistletoe; and next day the three young gentlemen insist on mounting the farm horses and carrying off the young ladies through the snow to their intended destination.

On the road they have a little difficulty at a ford which is frozen over. The litle child, who when a baby was left at the

'On the road they have a little difficulty at a ford which is frozen over'

inn in a very romantic way, is discovered by each of the elderly curmudgeons to be his own long-lost grandchild, and they have disputes as to her possession.

At last one of them quietly runs away with her on horseback. The other curmudgeons, feeling somewhat neglected, cheer themselves with buttermilk and port wine before parting, and in spite of a small regret or two, are happier in themselves and more genial towards their friends during all the following year.

A Very Different Christmas

RACHEL ILIFFE

In Victorian times life was hard and relentless in the industrial areas clustered along the banks of the River Severn in the Ironbridge Gorge. Even Christmas brought no relief from the constant noise, smoke and activity.

During the nineteenth century, Blists Hill was a hive of industrial activity, perhaps 400 to 500 people being employed by the industries occupying the site. The blast furnaces, built in the 1840s, would have produced an almost incessant pall of smoke, noise and heat. In 1851 the Brick and Tile Works came into production, further adding to the noise, smoke and activity.

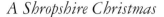

Both used the canal, built at the end of the eighteenth century, to transport goods and materials. In the 1870s, Lee Dingle Bridge was built and the whole site became covered with a mass of plateway lines. Through all this, mining, undoubtedly the first industry on the site, continued.

Christmas would have had little impact on all this activity. Christmas holidays, as we know them today, did not exist. Paid holidays were unusual for any manual worker before the 1880s; they did not become a legal entitlement until 1938. If you took a day's holiday, even for Christmas, it was unpaid. Even for those willing to forgo a day's pay, there was no guarantee that their employer would let them have the day off.

Things are very different at Blists Hill now. With the new century the industry declined. First to go were the blast furnaces, blown out in 1912; the last being the Brick and Tile Works which finally ceased its much reduced operation in the 1950s. They are now the quiet industrial monuments that form the basis of the Blists Hill Open Air Museum.

'The whole site became covered with a mass of plateway lines'

There are now other buildings here as well, the domestic and commercial properties that the museum has reconstructed on the site, and the industries that have been re-introduced, all building towards a small town as it might have been in about 1900.

Here we do mark Christmas. Christmas cards, first introduced in the 1840s, sit on the doctor's mantelpiece. There are also other traditional decorations, principally evergreens. These have been used in winter celebrations since pre-Christian times. The arrangement of them can vary considerably from simple boughs placed on flat surfaces to sophisticated sways and wreaths of evergreens made up to drape round the walls and across the ceiling. Sometimes individual laurel leaves are fastened to tape and then attached to the wall in a lattice pattern. Sometimes we also have a small Christmas tree here, decorated with cotton wool snow, plaster figures, pieces of

Only the snow is real in this scene posed at Blists Hill Museum.
The sawmill is on the left; the candle factory on the right

ribbon and Union Jacks. Poorer households might have managed nothing more than a few pieces of evergreen.

We have, from time to time, had Christmas events at Blists Hill, such as choirs singing in the street and 'Father Christmas'. Now most of these activities are concentrated at Coalport, where a magnificent 'Santa's Grotto' is built afresh each year around a central theme with associated entertainment; one year 'Alice in Wonderland', another year a circus with jugglers and stilt-walkers.

At Blists Hill we attempt to represent the true traditions of Christmas which, for the vast majority of Victorians, was hard work and little leisure!

Times Gone By

Salopian Shreds and Patches, *reprinted from* Eddowes' Journal, *is described as 'a repository for trifles'. The extracts that follow were selected in a very arbitrary fashion to give some impression of Christmas in years gone by.*

Christmas Festivities in Ancient Shrewsbury

23 December 1874
Archdeacon Owen tells us that 'in ancient days the Corporation of Shrewsbury was renowned for their sumptuous

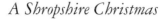

It is many years since snow has lain like this on Longden Road,
Shrewsbury

feasts on the election and swearing in of the Bailiffs, and other
public occasions, particularly at Christmas'. He thinks that it
was their custom to attend early matins on Christmas Day, in
state, either at St Mary's or St Chad's Church, which were
splendidly illuminated for the occasion. Thence they returned
in procession, accompanied by many of the inhabitants, to the
Guild Hall, where a breakfast of roast beef, brawn, mince
pies, ale etc. was provided. In 1540, it was ordered 'that the
breakfasts given by the Bayliffs on Christmas day, between
mattyns and hyghe mass, be no longer usyd, for diverse
consyderascions'. At a still later period, our Elizabethan poet
speaks of 'great and costly banquetting in Christmas'.

    R.E.D.

Christmas Dole at Worthen

24 December 1884

Fifty years ago, the farmers of Worthen and the neighbourhood used to distribute wheat at Christmas to poor women, mostly from the hilly districts of the adjoining parish of Pontesbury. As they came in considerable numbers, only a small quantity – a saucerful or so – was given to each person, but by the time they had been round all the houses, their bags contained a heavy load.

Proud Salopian

Christmas Fare at a Shropshire Hall – 26 December 1883

The provision for Christmas in 1576 at Longford may be supposed to have been accompanied by the Wassail Bowl (although no special allusion is made thereto), it being in universal use at that period.

A refinement of manners has, in a great measure, abolished the hospitality then customary in the baronial halls, but many examples still remain of old English festivity. The lovers of manly and rural sports, of the song and dance, of social intercourse and mutual happiness continue to look forward to Christmas with every prospect of enjoyment.

The Christmas carol and mince pies, which by some are supposed to be typical of the offerings of the Wise Men who came from afar to worship, bringing spices etc., still retain full sway as in the days of yore. The members of widely separated families travel long distances to gather around the Christmas fireside.

J.T.

A Christmas in the Weald Moors

29 December 1886

Miss Meteyard, a Shrewsbury woman, whose writings are too well-known to need any mention here, published in Chambers' Journal for 1884 a very interesting account of a visit to Preston Hospital in the previous year, the winter of which was a remarkably severe one. On New Year's Eve she received a message that a kinsman from Liverpool was coming, so great preparations were made for his reception. Amongst other good things there was to be a grand Christmas pudding, but at the last moment no eggs could be found. The time was late, but the moon shone brightly, and she resolved to start in search of some. She thus described her journey:

'To village and farmhouse doors we went; our appearance in some cases creating quite a wonder; but nobody had any eggs to spare, for everybody was going to have a pudding. Yet the walk and what we saw would have made up for much greater disappointment. Such pleasant warm homes; such pretty rustic festivals; such jugs of home-brewed ale; such crab-apples dancing on the top; such steaming puddings, and pies, and roasts; such gossip; such merry children; such cheerful old men and aged dames – these with the deep snow outside, the wild, solitary country, the distant forge fires roaring on and on, made a whole such as no pen can describe.

In most cases we were hospitably asked in – in some to taste the cheer. At last, after wandering through the deep snow of a primitive little orchard, whose russet tints and crystal rivulet I had in autumn-days stayed many times to see, we came to a small farmhouse and were admitted into a kitchen where a wood-fire roared up a chimney centuries old.

However bad the weather you will almost always meet someone out
walking along Victoria Avenue in The Quarry, Shrewsbury

A little new-born baby, its newly risen mother, and the father and grandparents, were gathered round, and being invited to the fire we admired the baby, when we not only got what we sought, but also a jug of hot spiced elderberry wine, against the tasting of which no negative would be taken. This little episode over and many grateful thanks given, we returned home, and I finally elaborated the great pudding as our aged alms-woman and quaint bachelor chatted beside the pleasant hearth.'

Wrekin

Family Life

RACHEL JONES

Rachel Jones wrote an account of family life in Whitchurch in the last years of the nineteenth century. The record was intended for her children but has a particular interest to a much wider audience because Rachel's brother, known in the family as 'Jim', was better known elsewhere as the composer Edward German.

One character that stands out distinctly was our family doctor, by name Brown, who was a Scotsman. He had a large countryside practice and was respected by rich and poor alike. We five little Joneses had the usual list of children's ailments, so he was a frequent visitor, and we looked upon him more as a friend than a doctor. After the patient was finished with, he would seat himself comfortably in an armchair, and tell stories

— some of them very tall ones — of his fishing and other adventures up in Scotland, and when he came to the climax, he would take a pinch of snuff, then give a prolonged chuckle peculiarly his own — Jim used to imitate him exactly. He would sit yarning by the hour, and sometimes, when his man called for him to an urgent case, he would deliberately finish his story, take his snuff, and go chuckling away as unconcerned as possible. . . .

Occasionally we went to the Browns' house in Dodington for tea, and that was a state occasion, for we felt they were of the 'upper classes' and we had to behave accordingly. The three Brown boys were for a long time Jim and Cliff's great chums but somehow Mab and I always detested them. Still we all had great fun together with summer picnics and skating on Brown Moss in the winter.

And the Christmas parties! I remember Mother giving one in the Browns' house, which for some reason was empty at the time — it was owned by Aunt Eliza and was a fine old rambling residence, said to be haunted which, of course, added to our joy.

Here we were able to entertain all the children we knew with a huge Christmas tree and everything complete. As far back as I can remember Jim was fascinated with the theatre and at our various parties gave performances with a miniature one we had from London. He was also a very good conjurer — in fact, he was always before the public in one way or another.

I think the happiest parties of all were at John Elliott's (later Dr Elliott of Chester) home. It was a little house up St Mary's Street but it was just given up to the wildest fun and Christmas jollity. We always had charades, which usually resolved into an extempore play by Jim and John Elliott, who seemed born to act together — John with a dry Rutland Barrington sort of humour and Jim equal to anything.

Of course all the houses in those times were decorated for

Christmas, and we kiddies were busy for days making mottoes on red flannel with cotton wool letters, and hung our stockings up until we were quite old – still the glamour was there just the same. When we lived at The Laurels, the town band used to come and play in the kitchen, nearly blowing the roof off – and I mustn't forget Harry, the ragman, who had a carol all of his own about 'Where Jasus lay'. It was a wild Celtic strain without time or tune – he just wandered on at his own sweet will. Every year he came with the same weird strains until he died and the carol went with him. We shall never hear the like again.

And a Famous Brother

SIR EDWARD GERMAN

Sir Edward German (1862–1936) was a prolific and successful composer, probably best remembered now for the light opera Merrie England. *Throughout his career his strong family ties kept him in touch with his home town. In 1882 he was obviously looking forward to spending Christmas there. . . .*

Dear Gals,
Very sorry not written but no time honestly no time. I have bought two tutty [*sic*] tambourines. . . . Glad you have

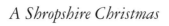

Edward German: 'Throughout all my work I think of nothing but
coming home'

written the play. I know it is good. I trust I have got a good and 'funny in the extreme' part. I am going to bring Mother a beautiful bit of Stilton. I sent Cliff {brother Clifford} a diary on his birthday. That reminds me, I must get one. I must get Mab {sister Mabel} brushes and white paint. The tambourines are jolly little things. Have been at Wimbledon teaching today instead of Monday – had to go to Bedford Concert. Am playing at Hereford on 30th. Oh! shan't I be jolly glad to get home. Oh!!!! I shall buy white whiskers for my part. . . . It may not be very unlike a well known doctor whose name begins with B {Dr Brown}. I ought to be an old codger who is always telling little anecdotes that have no meaning in them whatever. My great saying ought to be 'Ah!! talking of (so and so) reminds me of a little story' etc. If I don't write you you *will* know it's because I practically have no time. Throughout all my work I think of nothing but coming home and seeing you. . . so you can rest assured it is not because I forget you. I'll compose a little gipsy chorus when I come home.

Best love to each and all.

Your loving brother

Jim

To Mother –
Christmas, 1920

MARY WEBB

*Mary Webb wrote novels in which 'there was a lot of hot breath
and purple prose'. She was born in Shropshire in 1881 and her
love of the county and its countryside were inspirations for
novels such as* Precious Bane *and* Gone to Earth. *She also
wrote poetry, such as this Christmas offering.*

Within the doorway of your room tonight
I stood, and saw your little treasures all
Set out beneath the golden candle-light,
While silver chimes haunted the evenfall.
Here was the robin, very round and bright,
Painted by one of us with fingers small,
And childish presents, bought with grave delight,
For many an ancient Christmas festival.
And while I looked, dear mother, I thought of those
Great dreams that men have dreamed – music like flame,
The lovely works of many a deathless name,
Poetry blooming like a fragrant rose;
And knew God kept them in His house above,
As you our gifts, from the greatness of His love.

from

A House That Was Loved

KATHERINE KENYON

The house in question is Pradoe, near Oswestry, which is still a much-loved Kenyon family home. Katherine Kenyon was born in 1887 and died in 1981. She wrote the book to fill the long evenings of the black-out during the Second World War. It includes this description of the family Christmases of her childhood.

At Christmas-time a bullock was killed and given to the tenants. I remember standing beside my uncle and watching the women with white-covered baskets on their arms, coming up one by one as their names were called, curtsying, and choosing the joint they fancied. Mrs Jones, the bailiff's wife, hesitated for a long time between the heart and a sirloin.

'Come, Mrs Jones, you must make up your mind,' said my uncle at last, and she chose the heart. I imagined she was torn between desire for the big joint and the polite rule taught us in the nursery: 'Never take the biggest of whatever is offered you,' and I correspondingly admired her for her choice. . . .

Another one of the Christmas-time [memories] is of the boar's head. This used to stand on a little round table by

itself, the dish resting on a raised carved platter. It was thickly glazed all over, held an orange in its mouth, and had glass marbles with twisty insides for the eyes. I used to feel incredulous that anyone could eat it. I do not know why I was ever in the dining-room at breakfast-time at an age when I breakfasted in the nursery. But I clearly remember a sunny morning and Mr Fred How cutting himself slices from the back of the head and saying how good it was.

The Christmas tree was always in the library, its tip almost touching the ceiling, and its bulk taking up a large part of the room beyond the pillars. A curtain was hung between these, so that we should not see the tree as we passed to and fro from the dining-room. How splendid it was when at last the great moment arrived and we entered to find the curtain gone and beheld the thrilling and beautiful object! It would be twinkling with candles and lavishly hung with glittering

Pradoe: The house that was – and still is – loved

balls and ornaments, and round the base would be piled parcels of every size and shape. Soon the drugget-covered carpet would be littered with paper, and the air filled with the odour of warm wax and of extinguished candles, as they were put out one after another when they had burnt down nearly to the branches.

To me no other Christmas tree I have seen anywhere can compare with those that used to take up so much room in the little library. The strands of sparkly stuff that so often drape them nowadays seem to me all wrong, and of course, electric bulbs, though so much safer, are not as lovely as the living, twinkling flames. There was the excitement, too, when you were older, of watching them grow very small, and perhaps of putting them out yourself. These later trees were for the sake of other children. I remember hearing Lady Congreve urging her youngest boy to put out a candle with his fingers. Somewhat reluctantly he stepped forward and did it. 'Brave boy!' she said as he returned to her side, and I thought how warm and lovely it must be to receive such approval – the son, too, of a VC father! This may have been the year before the war, in which the eldest son, Billy, was to win the VC too.

We used to play spillikins and solitaire (I can remember some of the marbles intimately now) in the drawing-room with the unmarried aunts also staying there for Christmas. There was a piece of furniture which consisted of two small armchairs facing each other, with a little round table, rising from a single leg, between. It was on this table I loved if possible to play. It seemed a cosy bit of furniture. I remember there was a firescreen made out of a heron close by, and the whole lamplit atmosphere of the drawing-room used to envelop us graciously. Near the fire at the further end of the room the rest of the grown-ups would be sitting, reading, sewing or chatting in desultory fashion, hidden from us by the massed bank of chrysanthemums.

On New Year's Day in Shropshire no female may visit any cottage before noon for she would bring bad luck with her. This is firmly fixed in my mind because all unwittingly we were taken on one 1 January to see Mrs Jones, the bailiff's wife. As we came to the stile at the bottom of the field leading to the back of her cottage she came hurrying down the garden path waving her arms and uttering shrill cries. We stayed where we were, some on one side of the stile, some on the other, while she stood at her wicket and poured forth cries of prohibition and lament. I could not understand what it was all about, only I perceived with some dismay that Mrs Jones, who always said she loved to see us, did not want us to come a step nearer, and that she was very angry and very unhappy. All that I actually distinguished among the shrill cries that floated across the field was a continually repeated lament for her pigs. So we turned silently and went back again. The question of pigs puzzled and rather alarmed me. There seemed something sinister about it. What had they to do with us? – we never went near the cottage pigsties (which used to smell horribly). And it was all so different from the Mrs Jones we knew, dignified, and often tearfully sentimental, with her geraniums in the window and the Bible and *Uncle Tom's Cabin* on the table in front (though this, now I come to think of it, must be a later memory). It was long afterwards, hearing my parents tell of this Shropshire superstition, that I realized that Mrs Jones had been visited by a woman on a previous New Year's Day, and her sow had died shortly afterwards. Only by her unprecedented haste (she was a big, slow-moving woman) and unaccustomed violence of speech, had she averted another disaster from falling on her house the day she turned us back from coming to wish her a Happy New Year.

Letters Home

WILFRED OWEN

Wilfred Owen, who was born in Oswestry, was arguably the greatest writer Shropshire has ever produced. His literary skills were honed on the battlefields of France during the First World War. His war poems are some of the most powerful and moving ever written. His mother kept every letter Wilfred ever wrote to her. Those from Christmas 1915 are from a young man, recently enlisted and not too worried about anything – except getting home for Christmas.

What a difference a year makes! In January 1917 Wilfred was at the Front, where just to be warm and dry was luxury. Wilfred Owen's brief life ended at the Oise-Sambre Canal near Ors on 4 November 1918. News of his death reached his home in Shrewsbury on 11 November 1918 – Armistice Day. He was twenty-five years old. He left behind such magnificent and memorable poems as 'Anthem for Doomed Youth' and 'Dulce Et Decorum Est'.

Tuesday {21 December 1915}

Dearest Mother,

Your two letters came together yesterday! Up to an hour ago I still hoped for Leave over Christmas Day, but no longer think it likely. Yesterday I couldn't write for the same reason that I can't say much today. Thus. On Saturday I noticed three Boy Scouts about camp, and out of the bounty of my affections

gave them tea and biscuits at the Y.M.C.A. This is my reward: two of them asked me to come to their houses. I went yesterday to the first; but can't tell you all about them. In a word they are an excellent family (Girl 18, Boy 13, Boy 11, Girl 8), who take pleasure in inviting and feasting soldiers. They are Welsh in origin, and the circumambience of their home is as nearly akin to Mahim [Owen's family home in Shrewsbury] as possible!

Tonight I am going to a fairly large house, and the kid is waiting for me this moment, to catch the horse bus which is to take us there.

I am to eat Christmas Dinner with the first family (Williams) if I don't get Leave.

But one of the boys has already asked me to a kind of House Party with him, in the sad event of my not getting home. Am pretty sure to know for certain tomorrow, and shall write in any case.

Your own Wilfred

Leslie wants me to go to Bath for a day or two in my Holiday. So do I if I can get a glimpse of Johnny and Bobby there.

Postcard to his mother postmarked 23 December 1915:

No news of Christmas Leave which is bad news. Yet sorrow not. We shall have a merry time even in the Hut, and I am sure you will like to know I am in the bosom of a family at dinner-time! I *must* take a present with me for Raymond. Could you send me the brand-new Pocket Book secreted in my pigeon-holes? I had a good time yesterday: Pa & Ma ordinary, but darlin' little chilluns. Can Father get me a Pass to Shrews. via Bath, *if I travel in mufti*. If not, I shall need ressurees. Do you consent to a day or so in Bath? I have

written to Johnny on the strength of it! Men have gone out tonight to buy decorations for the Shanty. Thank Seatons for Xmas Card. Don't make up my bed, I will bide with Colin. Keep the Feast on the 25th. I am pretty sure to be with you for New Year's Day.
Dearest love to all
W.E.O.

Thursday {23 December 1915}

Dearest of Mothers,

I have had no letters today. I believe there is a muddle in the P.O. this year, but I hope you will get this by Christmas Day. The certainty is absolute: I shall be here over the 25th, with the majority of my Hut, and, indeed, of my Company. The latest rumour is that we shall not be allowed to get out of camp till we have fairly eaten our Christmas dinner under its auspices. Anyhow we shall feast rarely. Donaldson is giving us two birds (geese or turkeys) and there will be any number of plum-puddings. We are allowed 1*s* 6*d* per head extra pay for the day, which is funded and spent on delicacies and drinks. You will be pleased to hear that no spirits will be allowed at table. The best of it is we are all pleased.

I may go to the Williams later in the day, or on Boxing Day. Both Scouts have their lunch in my Hut now, instead of the Q.M. stores, where they are alone or with alien men. It is remarkable how their presence kills bad language, for the time. The restraint is beautiful, but if the novelty wears off and usual conditions are gone back to I shall turn out the kids.

We had a lecture this afternoon on bombs, from an expert. We shall begin firing after New Year.

I am being waited for now to go into Romford and buy special provisions. One has gone to London for the turkeys. I wonder what you will be having. It is galling to be kept away

from home for no useful reason, but it is not as if I were far away or long away. I really think to start on Tuesday or Wednesday.

Goodwill let there be; but Peace is a word that jars today and a word for hushed breath. I shall write continually, but this poor sheet may be the one to carry you my dear Christmas wishes the most ardent and solemn of any year yet. Wilfred x

At Christmas 1916 Wilfred Owen was on embarkation leave. He went to France on 30 December 1916 and into the line at Bertrancourt on the 9 January 1917 – when he wrote this letter.

My own dear Mother,

I forget both the day and the date. It is about the 9th. We moved further up yesterday, most of the way on 'buses.

I have just had your long-looked-for letter. It seems wrong that even your dear handwriting should come into such a Gehenna as this. There is a terrific strafe on. Our artillery are doing a 48-hours bombardment. At night it is like a stupendous thunderstorm, for the flashes are quite as bright as lightning.

When we arrived at this deserted Village last night, there had been no billets prepared for the Battalion – owing to misunderstanding. Imagine the confusion! For my part I discovered, or rather my new chosen and faithful servant discovered a fine little hut, with a chair in it! A four-legged chair! The roof is waterproof, and there is a stove. There is only one slight disadvantage: there is a howitzer just 70 or 80 yards away, firing over the top every minute or so. I can't tell you how glad I am you got me the ear-defenders. I have to wear them at night. Every time No. 2 (the nearest gun) fires, all my pharmacopaeia, all my boots, candle and nerves take a

smart jump upwards. This phenomenon is immediately followed by a fine rain of particles from the roof. I keep blowing them off the page.

From time to time the village is shelled but just now nothing is coming over. Anyhow there is a good cellar close to.

I am Orderly Officer today and stamp all the Battalion's letters. This has taken an age, and I have only a minute or two before I must despatch the Post.

I chose to spend an hour today behind the guns (to get used to them). The Major commanding the Battery was very pleasant indeed. He took me to his H.Q. and gave me a book of poems to read as if it were the natural thing to do!! But all night I shall be hearing the fellow's voice: Number Two – FIRE!

Please send the compass to: 2 Manchester Regt. B.E.F. I also need 50 Players Cigarettes and some plain chocolate. There is nothing in all this inferno but mud and thunder.

I am quite incapable of reading anything but your letters; and as you see nearly incapable of writing. Tell me every detail about Colin and Harold that you can; and of course, I long to know everything that happens – or does not happen – at home. Please tell Leslie and everybody that I really have not time nor wits to write them from under the cannon's mouth.

But it will lull shortly. I am quite well, and have plenty to eat. I get more and more used to the cold and wet.
Dearest love, my sweet Mother
from your Wilfred

I want a large, soft sleeping helmet and refills for the lamp. S.V.P.

Yule-tide Pastimes in the Country

'PROUD SALOPIAN'

Country people have always believed in hard work but plenty of play. In the days long before videos and Christmas specials on the television, they had no problem making their own entertainment, as this extract proves. It is credited to 'Proud Salopian', a regular contributor to Salopian Shreds and Patches.

In the good old times, when masters and servants took an interest in the welfare of each other, the hard work of the year gave place at Christmas to jovial merry-making. The favourite pastime was dancing, and farmhouse maidens, arrayed in their smartest gowns and gayest ribbons, displayed themselves to be duly admired by their mistresses, before hastening to the nearest village, to dance with might and main to the fiddler's strains. The 'kissing bush', a bunch of evergreens or mistletoe, bedecked with ribbons and fruit, was hung in the kitchen, or hall. A damsel in an exceptionally unrelenting household once complained that: 'It dunna look much like Chris'mas, nod a bit o' 'olly an 'ivvy, let alone a kissin'-bush. Scrat an' clane an' cook, is all our folks thinken on.'

Another who had been to a party, where there was no dancing, said, in answer to an inquiry as to how they amused themselves: 'W'y we played'n at turn the trancher and blind-man's buff till we wun tired, an' then begun to tell ridlesses,

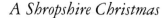

Playing blind-man's buff

an' whad twix puzzlin' to find 'em out, and then cryin' the weds, we gotten to three o'clock i'th' mornin'.'

The 'ridlesses' were puzzles or conundrums, and perhaps, at this festive season, I may be permitted to give a few of these specimens of rustic humour:

1.
Behind the bush, behind the thorn,
I heard a stout man blow his horn,
He was booted and spurred, and stood with pride,
With golden feathers by his side,
His beard was flesh, his mouth was horn.
I am sure such a man could never have been born.

2.
Long legs, short thighs,
Little head, and no eyes.

3.
Down in yonder meadow I have a troop of white horses –
now they go, now they go, now they stand still.

Answers:
1. A cock. 2. A pair of tongs. 3. The teeth.

For much of the foregoing information, I am indebted to
that treasury of all matters connected with old Salopian
country life, Miss Jackson's *Shropshire Word Book*.

from

Friends Round the Wrekin

LADY CATHERINE MILNES GASKELL

*This is a fairy story. It was recounted by Lady Catherine
Milnes Gaskell in her book* Friends Round the Wrekin,
*published in 1914. The book tells of Shropshire's heroes,
heroines, folk-lore and traditions. It looks back to a time when
all entertainment was home-made and story-tellers were held in
the highest regard – especially at Christmas! (Bess is Lady
Catherine's young daughter.)*

After the rain and the cold, a day of brilliant sunshine. A white rime lay over meadow and lawns, birds hovered by the windows in expectation of food. A few hours later the frost vanished, and Bess and I went out into the garden. Suddenly old Burbidge hobbled up to me: 'The great white 'uns are on the wing,' he cried excitedly. And there I saw the swans and their progeny flying round and round in ever larger and larger circles. My old gardener looked on grimly.

'Did you ever hear of Silena Grattan?' he asked. 'She used to tell wonderful stories of birds and fishes when my sister Nell and I was childers. She lived at Wyke.'

'Did she tell you any stories about swans?'

'She did when she came to farmer Thomas's Yule-tide games and dances.'

'Do tell us,' said Bess.

'Well, it was this way. Silena, you must know, mam, was a bit of a cripple, so while the old played cards and the young ones danced Sir Roger de Coverley and the Tempest, she would sit on a stool before a log fire, gather the children round her and tell stories.'

'I want to hear them all,' said Bess.

'Not now,' said my old friend. 'I be too busy with the boys, but when 'tis dark and the sun's down and the stars shining I will come in if you will, miss, and tell you summat, if so be as I can remember the old tales.'

After tea Bess and I sat in the Chapel Hall. Suddenly there was a loud knock at which one of the great hounds jumped up with a growl, then yawned and lay down when she saw who was our guest.

'The stories,' explained old Burbidge.

Bess made him sit down by the fire. 'Tell us about the swans,' she said.

'Aye, aye, miss,' said old Burbidge, ''twas always the story of the seven swans that I loved best myself.'

Then he went on: 'Now it seems that there was once upon a time a king, and that king had a beautiful wife, and seven sons and one little girl. And one day the queen said to the king: 'Sweetheart, lend my thy white horse that I may go fox-hunting.' So the king said, 'Thou art welcome, only do not try to ford the Severn for the floods are out, and the waters are great, and the spirits of the rivers and the lakes have great power at such times.' Then the queen promised to do as her husband wished, and the king lent her his snow-white steed. All went well. The little princes all rode with their mother on chestnut and bay ponies. Only the little daughter remained at home with her father, she being too young to hunt, it was said.

'All went well till the huntsmen turned homewards. Now it seems they had all had a merry day, and killed two foxes on the Long Mynd, but the darkness came upon them swiftly, and they were afraid they would lose their way. 'Let us swim the Severn,' said the queen, forgetting her promise to the king. So she and her seven sons plunged into the water. Whereupon the spirits of the deep waters came and charmed them and dragged them down, and a witch turned the queen and her horse into a grey rock, but the prince boys she turned into seven swans, and the seven ponies into seven frogs.

'Now, when the huntsmen got back to the palace the king was very sad when he heard what had happened, and he caused a proclamation to be written, saying that he would give half his kingdom to any witch, magician, or enchantress, who would turn the grey rock back into his queen and the white steed, and who could change the seven swans back into his sons.

'Now for all that the king was a mighty man and had many servants and many subjects, he had to wait many years till this could be done. When the princess was of marriageable age,' continued my old friend, 'there came to her one day, as

In 1917 these youngsters were messing about on the river

she was walking through the woods, a poor lame hare. "How were you hurt, hare?" asked the princess. "A wicked man shot me with a bow and arrow," said the beast; whereupon the princess took off her own kerchief from her breast and bound up the poor beast's paw. The hare thanked her, and said, "Come back at midnight and I will tell you something to your advantage."

'Then, it seems,' said Burbidge, 'that the princess got out of her bed when the stars were shining. And she dressed all in white, and she walked out, and she walked and she walked, till she got to the heart of the wood, the great Edge-wood, they say. And there she saw the little people dancing; and flying round and round the tree tops were the seven great birds, her brothers. As she stood looking, there came running up to the glade the hare, and in his mouth he held a branch of mistletoe. "Wear this in thy breast," he said.

'And then the princess remembered it was Christmas night; and in the place of the hare was a beautiful child, and she put

78

out her arms, and behold the child and the hare were both gone; but the swans had alighted, and in the place of the great white birds stood the seven princes.

'Then they all went to the rock by the Severn, and the princess laid the mistletoe upon it, and straightaway it changed into the queen; but one of the horse's feet she forgot to touch, and one lock of the queen's hair. So the horse's foot remained grey, but the lock of the queen's hair became a jewel which the queen wore all the rest of her life. As to the frogs, the little people caught them and turned them back to ponies. There is one night in June, but I canna' be sure which 'tis, when the boys used to go out frog-catching. Old Sally Mayland used to say, with a laugh, 'twas a cheap way of buyin' a horse. But there may be worse!'

A few minutes later old Burbidge rose from his chair. 'It does one good to talk of the things that one heard as a little lad,' he said and he got up and went out.

'What a lot of really interesting things Burbidge knows,' said Bess. I could not help feeling it was a pity that the power and gift of telling stories has died out, for a story told remains with a child to manhood and after, whereas the charm of a book is often fleeting, and as easily forgotten as a dream.

Shropshire Folk-lore

CHARLOTTE BURNE

In this, a second extract from Charlotte Burne's comprehensive study of Shropshire folk-lore, she talks about traditional Christmas entertainments.

The custom of offering a mince pie and a glass of wine or ale to all visitors who may come to a house during Christmas, no matter at what hour in the day, is still kept up by old-fashioned families. There is a 'luck' about mince pies, and it is this. For every house in which any person eats a mince pie during the Twelve Days, he will enjoy a happy month in the ensuing twelve months. Nowadays people begin to say that the 'happy months' depend on the number of mince pies eaten before Christmas, but the true old superstition is as I have given it, and is but a detail of the grand principle that on the events of the Twelve Days of Christmas depend the fortune of the ensuing twelve months. . . .

One day among the Twelve is a day of evil omen, namely Innocents' Day, the 28 December, otherwise called 'Cross Day'. The ancient sages of Pulverbatch applied this name not only to Innocents' Day itself, but throughout the year to the

day of the week on which it had last fallen, which was counted an unlucky day for the beginning of any work or other undertaking. 'It must have been begun on Cross Day' was a proverbial saying applied to any unfortunate enterprise.

With this one unpleasant exception, the days went merrily on. The farm and household work were as far as possible laid aside, though cooking and baking necessarily went on in extra measure. The servants each 'went a-Christmasing', i.e. visited their homes during the season, and while at their masters' houses were allowed to spend much of their time in working for themselves. In the evening fireside games, riddles, cards and dancing took the place of the ordinary occupations of spinning and winding. Blind-man's buff was the favourite game of the juniors, rivalled only by 'sousing for apples', or taking apples out of a tub of water with the teeth, the hands being tied behind the back, and comrades on the alert to souse the bold wight's head under water just at the critical moment.

Guests, too, there were, of all degrees, and among them, besides the private friends of the family, invited or uninvited, the carol singers must be reckoned. They still flourish, though they have changed with the times. . . .

It seems as if no mid-winter feast in any county could be complete without its masquerade. In Shropshire we have two distinct varieties of these disguised and unbidden guests: the morris-dancers of south and west Shropshire, whose performance consists only of dancing and sometimes singing; and the so-called morris-dancers of the north-eastern quarter, in Staffordshire more accurately termed guisers. A company of these performers goes yearly about Newport or Edgmond and the country around, enacting what is nominally the legend of St George, but is really the world-old drama of the seasons, of strife, and death, and renewed life. In the olden days, so I have been told by an eye-witness, at the first alarm of their

approach, all the household hurried to bar the door, and if they were not in time to do so, in rushed the rabble rout of masquers without leave asked or given, and interlarded their performance with all sorts of antics and mischievous pranks. Finally, when the last player 'little Jack Devil Dout' (dout = to do out, to extinguish a fire) pronounced his threat of 'sweeping them all into the grave', they proceeded with mock energy to sweep up the hearth, but in reality to scatter the sticks and make the dust fly all abroad. . . .

The Christmas festivities of north Shropshire farmhouses must always have been greatly impeded by the fact that the servants all keep the Christmas holiday at their own homes, leaving their places the day after Christmas Day, and

Snow scene in The Quarry, Shrewsbury

returning to them, or going to new ones, the day after New Year's Day. During the intervening week, the cottages are crowded to their utmost capacity, or beyond it; and the scarcity of accommodation often leads to the greater part of the family sitting up by the fireside occupied with games and music the whole night through, after what, it is probable enough, may have been the primitive practice of the revellers round the Yule-fire.

On Plough Monday, the Monday after Twelfth Day, ploughing and spinning begin again. Indulgent masters allowed a half-holiday on this day. The extra allowance of beer was stopped and the maids would joke the waggoner on the small size of the wooden bottle he took out to the field, at which he would draw his sleeve across his eyes in mock distress, saying, 'Ah, it's Sorrowful Monday for me!'

At Candlemas, the winter season was considered to have ended, and the Christmas holly and ivy were taken down on Candlemas Eve, and not till then, a custom still faithfully observed both in churches and houses. I have been told of an old servant in south Shropshire who was always at great pains to replace them with snowdrops, the Purification flower, which are usually considered unlucky. Old-fashioned people were careful how they disposed of the withered evergreens. They were never thrown away, for fear of ill-luck following, but were either burnt in the house-fire or eaten by the milch-kine, and considering the almost sacred associations which cling around the familiar holly and ivy, there could hardly be a more remarkable link between the English Christmas of today and the primitive home-festival of our Aryan forefathers.

from

Burlton Village – A Recollection of Childhood

MARJORIE JONES

In 1989 Marjorie Jones wrote and published a short book about the history of Burlton, a village in the north of the county. The book includes the author's very detailed recollections of growing up on a farm in a country village in the early years of the twentieth century. In this extract she talks about family Christmases. (Nora is the author's half-sister and she also mentions her younger sister, Cissie.)

Preparations for Christmas occupied us, on and off, for about three months. We were encouraged, with little success on my part, to make presents for each other and for our parents; we made endless paper chains and other baubles for decorating the house and the Christmas tree. Nora made beautiful dolls of coloured crepe paper – masses of them representing fairies, children in nursery rhymes, those of other lands in national costume, grand ladies, queens, etc. Unfortunately all had to be female because they balanced on wide 'ballet skirts' and

had no feet. They were, nevertheless, very ingenious and pretty and were often given as presents from the tree. As the day approached mysterious parcels were surreptitiously bundled into the house and disappeared into our parents' room or on to very high shelves. Cissie was pretty good at discovering them, but as we never dared to unpack them it was a fairly fruitless though exciting exercise.

On Christmas Eve there was decorating the house, an activity which was not viewed with great enthusiasm by the adults. Until we were old enough we went with one of the farm boys to cut holly, ivy and what we called 'fir' branches from the orchard, garden and fields, and it was dumped in the little yard outside the back door until afternoon, when as many grown-ups as could reasonably do so, disappeared, so that we could wreak havoc on our own. Nora did, in fact, often organize us and make us clear up the indescribable mess afterwards. The result was not very imaginative but we were easily satisfied.

In the evening we hung up stockings over the fireplace in the kitchen. This was a necessary precaution for our parents because we tended to wake up soon after midnight and, not knowing the time, start rampaging about and keeping the whole household from its rest. A decree went out, therefore, that stockings could not be opened until 6.30 a.m. on pain of confiscation. Usually we did creep halfway down the kitchen stairs after everyone had gone to bed just to see if the stockings were bulging. The remainder of the night was spent dozing and giggling and chattering until an alarm went off, whereupon we lit our candles in a fever of excitement and crept down the stairs. How we weren't burnt to a cinder I shall never know, but as we had never had anything else but lamps and candles for illumination, we must have learnt very early to treat open flames with respect.

Electric torches were a fairly new phenomenon to us; we

called them flash lights and I remember that Cissie once had one in her stocking. She flashed it on all and sundry for an hour or so, whereupon it gave up the ghost, so by eight o'clock or whatever time it was that we were allowed to go into our parents' room, the poor thing was dead. When we were a little older we thought it rather clever and witty to sing 'Christians awake' outside our parents' bedroom – though it was hardly necessary to arouse them by that time – and we then flooded in with all our goodies, dumping them and ourselves on the large bed.

I get a great feeling of warmth and love about all this. My mother I loved dearly, but my father was a distant, rather terrifying figure who was not often at home, and with whom we associated naughtiness and spanking and a loud cross voice. He was not like this on Christmas Day. In retrospect this early morning bouncing on the bed and having fun with Daddy, has acquired a nice, cosy, relaxed atmosphere. How far I have imagined this since, I do not know.

I do not remember about going to church on Christmas Day – maybe this was the least of our excitements – but if there was no service at Burlton we would have to be driven to Loppington in the dog-cart, and our parents may not have wished to employ Astley, the waggoner and our usual driver, on Christmas Day. If we did go, it would have been with Nora, while Mother cooked the turkey. My father rarely went to church, although I think he was a believer in a bored sort of way. Mostly on Sunday mornings and on feast days he went on his bicycle to visit his half-brother Ted at Burlton Mill.

Christmas dinner, as for most children, was a terrific affair. After the turkey, there was the flaming pudding with holly on top and lots of silver sixpences and threepenny bits inside. Then there were nuts and sweets and an extremely replete feeling at the end of it. We were then banished for the afternoon while Nora and our parents sought a little peace

and relaxation from the turmoil. Nora always retired to her room on these occasions. She must have been quite young, barely twenty, so I don't imagine that she really needed to lie down but this is what we thought she did. We spent the afternoon playing with all our new toys; I remember particularly bricks (I had some extremely sophisticated bricks called gobbledy-goos which could be built into people), puzzles and painting books, and stuffing ourselves with the goodies which were left from our stockings. These, by tradition, always had a handful of mixed nuts in the toe, then an orange, an apple and sometimes a few sweets or a bar of chocolate. The rest of the stocking was filled with the things we had asked Father Christmas for. Presents from the family including aunts and cousins were exciting but nothing like as memorable as the contents of the stocking. I think that with

In 1917 the River Severn at Ironbridge was frozen hard enough to drive on. The Albert Edward Bridge is in the background

all the thrill of unpacking, handing over our own gifts, strewing paper and string all over the place, we were a little confused about who had given what to whom and when, a few days later, we were given the agonizing task of writing to our relatives, we often had to be helped to fit the right gift to the right person.

On Boxing Day there was The Party – and The Christmas Tree. (We never had the Christmas tree on Christmas Day.) The Party was for the children of our employees; counting all the casuals, these amounted to quite a number. There were five or six full-time farm workers, plus milking women and Mrs Fardoe who came to do the washing and 'run' the kitchen at evening adult parties. Sometimes there were younger sisters or brothers of the two maids.

At the Hall there was always a Treat early in January for all the children in the village, but there were distinct differences. All the children (except us, for some reason) had to take their own mugs; the food was mainly thick chunks of bread spread with jam, and bought sugar buns cut in half. After a few games we all trooped into the larder to see the Christmas tree and to receive our gifts. I have an idea that these were quite nice, but they have left no special impression. There was then a 'scramble' back in the kitchen, when nuts and sweets were scattered on the floor and you grabbed what you could. We were discouraged from taking a very active part in this, as it was considered very rough, which it was. Finally, we lined up at the door and were given an apple, an orange and a little bag of sweets.

At our party, the food was the thing – iced cakes, sugar cakes, chocolate cakes and biscuits, decorated jellies in little cases and two rather special things which I never see now – flat biscuits covered with very hard icing in white, pink or chocolate and, superimposed, an animal or bird in contrasting colour of icing. These were enormously popular as were the

'A.B.C.' biscuits – small plain biscuits in the shape of a letter of the alphabet; with these, if lucky, one could make one's own name or other interesting words. The children were not expected to bring their own mugs and were treated more like real guests than they were at the Hall, whose party smacked more of a 'charity treat'. I'm not sure whether we were aware of this, but if so I expect it was because our parents had put the idea into our heads.

Our Christmas tree was also in the larder, known as the milk house. It was more lavishly decorated than the one at the Hall, with lots of candles, fragile sparkling balls, silver tinsel and masses of Nora's paper dolls. All the little girls received one of these each year and I believe they were highly treasured. I don't remember what the boys had but I expect they were only small cheap toys. Then there were crackers which we didn't have at the Hall – though I think we had already had them on Christmas Day. Finally we sang the National Anthem before closing the party.

When the children had left, there was a massive clearing up operation, as everything had to be clean and tidy before the maids left for their annual two weeks' holiday. It was the traditional holiday time for indoor servants and quite sacrosanct. Even my mother, who was a charmer and much loved by all the maids I remember, could not persuade them to modify this very special right.

from

Memories of Clun

RONALD K. MOORE

*In the days before there was a television or radio in almost every
house, carol singers had an important role to play in spreading
the sounds of Christmas. At Clun they took their carol singing
seriously as Ronald K. Moore explains in his description of life
in the small south Shropshire town.*

The band, in various forms, naturally appeared at all
gatherings and would have been most hurt if they had not
been asked to turn out. On Armistice Day, however, the
gathering was in the church and, of course, this was the
organist, Mr Tong's domain. After some sharp words and
heated discussion, it was decided that the band and organ
would both feature in the church, so 'God our help in ages
past' was sung to the accompaniment of Mr Tong roaring
away with all the stops out, and the band, red-faced and
looking fit to burst, blowing for all they were worth in an
attempt to drown the organ. The congregation's piping efforts
were quite lost in the resulting deafening uproar.

If the band and organist appeared to be in a constant state
of rivalry, they were but beginners compared with the
competitive spirit to be found in the annual carol singing
groups. Around Christmas time in the 1920s small parties of
carollers could have been seen casually winding up trackways

The shell of Clun Castle stands out in the snow

to distant farms throughout the valley, singing to the accompaniment of a wheezy melodeon or squeaky fiddle and then walking on to another farm, but there was nothing casual about Clun carol singing in those days.

Well before Christmas, the leader of the group called on all the residents of his district, for like robins, each party had a territory. Sometimes this was hereditary and in other cases it was open to dispute, so it was the leader's job to visit possible new clients and 'take' the singing. Then, once this was sorted out, the serious business of practice could begin.

One year, 'Old Charlie's' party determined to include the new residents of Bleak Ridge, a hill farm just in their area. The two lady farmers had built a new wooden bungalow, large cattle sheds and poultry houses, and even brought in pedigree heifers. They could be lucrative clients for the carolling party, so the pre-Christmas call was duly made and the ladies became officially on Charlie's list of calls.

At last, Christmas approached and the big night arrived. So, after a few drops of something warming at The Crown in Church Street, the company moved on to The Sun – the major

A perfect period piece as Mary Ann Luther poses in the snow-covered Clun countryside

call in Clun itself — and then out into the frosty night air and the long trudge to Llanedric, The Bryn and Bleak Ridge. By now, the icy wind was bringing flurries of snow and the evening was drawing on as the little party struggled up the rough track to Bleak Ridge. Soon a large, well-lit wooden house loomed up. Charlie's party shuffled into position and sang lustily for 15 minutes. The programme completed, the door was knocked and the group stood in a respectful silence. After a long pause, a rustling sound was heard from behind the door. The singers looked at each other and wondered what to do. Further knocking produced only increased rustling, so while Charlie went around the back to find another door, 'Bert the Green' was quietly hoisted up to peep through one of the high windows. With an angry roar he leapt down. 'We've been singing to the — hens,' he bawled. It was a large hen house!

St Chads, Shrewsbury, in the snow

Recollections of the Old Welsh Frankton Carol Singers

TOM BORDERER

At Welsh Frankton there was a great tradition of carol singing but a very relaxed approach – possibly because of all the Christmas spirit involved!

The Welsh Frankton carol singers were an established institution in the parish when I went to live there in 1927. I cannot remember now just why I joined them, but it was certainly not on account of my vocal ability. On second thoughts I believe it was because I was a fiddler, and able to act as a kind of string precentor who could give the correct pitch to the carols.

The nucleus of the carollers was the church choir, but other interested singers fell in from time to time. The trebles were well in the majority, these including the piping juniors and a smattering of those, who lacking any sense of harmony, sang a treble part an octave lower. An occasional alto added variety, and at least one tenor, and maybe a couple of basses. But what

we lacked in musical balance was compensated for by unbounded enthusiasm for the job in hand. An appointed cashier carried a collecting box and what went into it was given to church funds, but the financial side of the venture took second place to the fun our excursions provided. The parish being a large one, it took three nights to complete the annual tour.

The main body of the carol party usually met outside the school but odd files who failed to join the initial parade fell in en route. There was a delightful air of inconsequence about everything, and no preconceived programme, so that it was left to someone to suggest where we should move off to first. Sometimes it would be to Lower Frankton, at other times Hardwick or Gannow was destined to feel the force of our initial assault. As far as I can remember we were never partisan over where we sang, and although there was a good percentage of dissenters in the parish, they always seemed pleased to accept and appreciate our efforts.

A strange thing is that although we never had a rehearsal everyone seemed to know the words and music of the carols we sang, and we had quite a varied repertoire. I can only imagine our carol singers did their Christmas homework very thoroughly. Of course, our repertoire included most of the well known carols but occasionally we put in a lesser known one. A favourite was 'Softly Falls The Winter Snow'. It is worthy of note that during the nine or ten years that I accompanied the carol singers I never remember any snow.

By the time I had joined the carol singers the villagers had got used to anticipating them, so there was no apparent surprise when we turned up. In the few big houses, outlying farms, and in the most modest cottages there always appeared to have been some preparation made for our visits. At the larger houses and at most of the farms we were regaled with the more orthodox Christmas fare, but at most of the cottages

the refreshments were almost entirely home-made, including the beer and the wines, which we found could easily disturb vocal stability, but in spite of this we always seemed able to fulfil all our obligations.

When we turned up at a rendezvous we sometimes sang outside the house, but we never went away without being asked inside for refreshments. Sometimes the door was thrown open to us and we performed inside while Christmas fare was conjured on to the table. Before we left, and after the exchange of much raillery and innocent leg pulling, a barrage of seasonal greetings was heard on all sides, and we moved off to our next Yule-tide engagement.

I can still picture our determined little band, lighted by storm lanterns, and full of the spirit of the season, trudging along the lanes from house to house, encouraged by the thought that wherever we stopped we should be welcomed. Our journeys were made easier and more enjoyable if there was a favourable moon, and on these excursions it was brought home to me how much our lives, compared with the lives of townspeople, are influenced by the 'parish lantern'. A mental picture that still remains vivid is that of Higher Perthy, with its irregular line of cottages nestled below their protecting bank, with windows showing yellow with lamplight. Neat little places they were without and within, and I remember several in which a family bible stood in a place of honour. Unhappy thought that a television set may now occupy the honoured place!

It would have been strange if some of our carolling excursions had not been fraught with incidents, and some unfortunate ones. One night another engagement prevented me setting out with the carol party, but my wife, who happens to be a fiddler too, volunteered to take my place. The party had sung at a few places on the way to New Marton, and eventually reached a farm there. Crossing the farmyard in

the dim light, my wife stepped into a shallow well. She fell in, and though she fortunately saved the fiddle from harm, she smashed my best bow. The next year misfortune befell the fiddle when one of our party kindly offered to carry it for me between calls. We were entering the back drive to Gannow Hill when the chivalrous one ran into an iron gatepost and knocked all the carol music out of the old instrument for that night at least.

When I first went out with the carol singers we travelled on foot, but later, through the kind auspices of the local bus proprietor, we had a bus in which to make our most distant calls. One night we had presented our modest programme at Hardwick Lodge and two singers, anxious to regain the shelter of the bus, dashed into an iron gate and needed considerable repairs before we could proceed on our 'musical ride'.

It is now nearly thirty years since my old fiddle and I joined Frankton carol singers, and winters have provided the odd white Christmas since then. Times have changed, and the oil lamps have gone from the cottages on Higher Perthy, for electricity has come to the whole village.

In these days carols come over the air at the pressing of a switch through the medium of radio and television, yet many of us remember, with pleasurable joy, the live shows of the days when village life had some links with the Merrie England of our forefathers.

Sam Evans' Christmas Carol

E.V. BAYNE

Unless we write down – or get someone else to record – our recollections and the stories we have to tell, they die with us and that is an incalculable loss. Fortunately this is the story of a special carol, the words of which, at least, have been recorded for posterity.

In the small village of Dudleston, near Ellesmere about a hundred years ago, little Sam Evans learned at his mother's knee a carol he was to remember all his life. In the good old days, carol singing on Christmas Eve and on Christmas morning played a definite part in celebrating Christmas, not only as a season of festivity but also in its true religious sense as the birthday of Christ.

The carol Sam learned was longer than most carols, but nevertheless he took some pains, as the years rolled by, to teach both words and music to one or two of his best friends, who secretly enjoyed the added prestige of singing a carol unknown to others in the neighbourhood. With one or another of these friends, as Christmas followed Christmas, Sam never failed to visit the gentry in their homes to sing to them this special carol on Christmas morning.

In his old age he remembered with particular pleasure

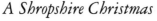

being invited with his friends into the presence of Sir John Kynaston of Hardwick to sing the carol. Sir John listened attentively throughout and, as the last cadence died away, he clapped his hands with delight. 'Sing it again, Sam, sing it again,' he urged, and, to the butler who answered his summons: 'Bring in the ale. Let these men drink, then we'll have it right through again.'

Sir John was not the only one interested in the carol. Sam Evans left Dudleston when he married and went to live in the parish of Cockshutt. He was a regular church-goer and though not a chorister, his excellent voice was a decided asset. It soon attracted the attention of the vicar, who, the following Christmas, heard for the first time, the carol of which Sam was so proud. It was he who encouraged Sam to write it down. In this Sam was helped by that kindly lady, Miss Gray of the Bridgewater Estate Office, in the early years of this century; she typed it and bound it into a neat little booklet with a blue cover tied with a blue silk cord. It is now the treasured possession of Sam's daughter.

Sam died in 1926 at the age of eighty-three. Unfortunately, Miss Gray did not record the author, nor the tune to which the carol was sung.

SAM'S CAROL
[An extract]

Come all you true, good Christians
Who liveth here on earth,
Let's celebrate the morning
Of our sweet Saviour's birth.
This is the happy hour,
It was this blessed morn
To save all souls from ruin
This Lamb of God was born.

Then soon the Angel Gabriel,
In Scripture it is said,
Went with his holy message
Unto a virgin maid –
'Thou blessed amongst all women,'
For he did greet her then
Saying 'Thou shalt be a mother
To the Saviour of all men.'
'Oh, then,' replied the virgin,
'How must I bear, or can
I now conceive a Saviour
When I never knew a man?'
'Oh, then,' replied the Angel,
'These things shall surely be,
The powers of the Almighty
Shall overshadow thee;
Rejoice at these glad tidings
Which cometh from the Lord.
And be it to thy hand-maid
According to thy word.'
When her time it was accomplished,
To Bethlehem she'd come,
And then this Blessed Virgin
Was delivered of a Son.
No prince or pomps attended,
His honour was but small;
A manger was his cradle
And his bed an ox's stall.

Letter to the Editor

*Anyone who has ever opened the front door to a group of
youngsters who, singing flat, manage half a verse of 'Once in
Royal David's City' before tailing off to the rattle of their
collecting tin, will sympathize with the writer of this letter
which appeared in* Eddowes' Journal *on 22 December 1880.*

Sir,

I invoke your powerful aid in the attempt to put down a
custom which, however laudable the origin of it may have
been, has of late years become an intolerable nuisance. I allude
to what is called 'carol singing', but which is rather carol
howling. Night at this season of the year is simply made
hideous by gangs of boys, girls and men, who infest our town
and suburbs and annoy the inmates of quiet families by
howling sacred words to what ought to be regarded as sacred
tunes in utter disregard of the meaning of the words, or
anything like harmony, and finish up the previous night's
offence by shouting under your windows early in the
mornings of Christmas and New Year's days their
congratulations. Apart from the blasphemy of the whole
proceeding, it is a disturbance of the public peace, and might
be so regarded by the appointed guardians of the same.
Yours etc.
A Lover of Quietness
Shrewsbury 20 December 1880

Down Memory Lane

W.L.M. FRANCIS

At ninety-six years old, 'Mac' Francis has many Christmas stories to tell. He has lived and worked for most of his life in Oswestry, except for his military service in the Tank Corps in the First World War during which he won the Military Medal. Here he looks back on his days in the family grocery business.

Christmas 1913 was the year of the best hams ever! The army captain who lived at Wood Hill told Mr Francis Senior (Mac's father) that he had some 20–25lb hams to sell. Apparently the herdsman had been clearing a loft and had found these hams, which must have been overlooked for about twenty years! They were covered with 'malt dust' and said to be first class eating – although they were hard on the outside, with quite a lot of waste.

Mr Francis Senior offered the Captain 8*d* per pound for them.

'Oh! Mr Francis,' said the Captain, 'I couldn't accept that!'

'Well,' said Mr Francis, 'if they are as good as you say, perhaps, we could go to 10*d*.'

But the Captain would have none of it: 5*d* per pound was quite enough, he said!

The hams proved to be best sellers and, according to Mac, tasted better than any ham he's tasted before or since.

On another occasion the Colonel from Park Hall Army Camp came into the shop just before Christmas and asked if the bakery attached to the business could bake Christmas cakes for his troops. He needed about two tons of cake in all! Mac well remembers delivering some of the cake to the camp by mule and trap – 6 cwt at a time. Although baked in such enormous quantities, the cake was first-class and as a result the shop was put on the official list of suppliers to the army and navy.

It was just before Christmas one year during the First World War that Mr Garrett from Worcester way, who travelled in jams for a company from the other side of

Turkey time in Market Drayton High Street in 1924

Malvern, called at the shop. At that time there was no jam to be had anywhere in Oswestry – and probably very little elsewhere in the county. The company Mr Garrett worked for had sold all its best jams and – unable to get staff or sugar – was to close for the duration of the war.

But Mr Garrett did have some apple mixture jams left – such as apple and raspberry, and apple and plum. If Mr Francis Senior would trust him with an open cheque, he could have as much as he liked.

Mr Garrett went off with the cheque and a few days later the station master at Oswestry – it was the Cambrian Railway in those days – rang to say there was 'a hell of a lot of casks waiting to be delivered to the shop'. It was the jam. Two drays-full, in fact. In all there were some 20 casks each containing seventy-two 2lb stone jars, and each jar was wrapped in straw and filled with apple mixture jams. As the unpacking progressed, casks – empty and full – and the straw out of them, stretched down Beatrice Street. The jars of jam sold for about $4\frac{1}{2}d$ each and went on sale at 10 a.m. By 2 p.m. a group of railway workers arrived from Crewe. They had heard about the jam and staggered off with six or even twelve jars each. By the end of the day, all but two or three of the casks of jam were sold!

Mac Francis still remembers those hard Christmases from about 1914 onwards when, as he says: 'there were a lot of poor people about'. Three or four of the butchers in the town would use any meat left over from Christmas to make delicious soup, 'the like of which you would seldom get from a tin today', to give free to anyone who wanted it.

In those days there would be a street market with sixty to a hundred stalls which sold 'every blessed thing' for days leading up to Christmas. Among the things you could buy from the stalls were geese, turkey, game, bacon and, of course, toys galore, some of which were 'a bit of a twist'

Christmas shopping in wartime Shropshire. No signs of shortages
here

while others were sheer magic. Mac longed for a jack-in-
the-box but had to wait three or four years before his father
bought him one.

It is hard to imagine in these days of frozen food of all
sorts, that the first big deep freezes appeared in shops,
enabling them to sell frozen food, in the very late 1950s.
With the arrival of a big deep freeze at the Francis' shop in
Cross Street, they started to stock frozen chickens – an

expensive, luxury food in those days. One customer asked Mac to put her a frozen chicken by for Christmas week. After Christmas, however, she came in to complain. The chicken, she claimed, had been very, very tough. Had she de-frosted it carefully? Oh, yes. And how had she cooked it? It turned out that she hadn't cooked it at all because she thought frozen food did not need any cooking!

There is one Christmas Eve that Mac Francis will certainly never forget – and that was in 1956. He was serving in the shop, which was packed with customers, when a gentleman walked in and insisted on seeing him in private. Thinking he was a traveller with some special line, Mac agreed to give him 'just two minutes', as the queues waiting to be served grew.

The gentleman said he was from *The People* and he had come to validate Mac's prize-winning entry for a crossword competition. In spite of the gentleman's protests that delay could cost him dear, Mac insisted that, prize or no prize, he wasn't going to let his customers down on Christmas Eve. The man from *The People* was sent around to Mac's home to wait. Several hours later Mac finally closed the shop and went home. The man was still waiting, after checking Mac's entry to ensure that it was all his own work, he finally announced that Mac had won £1,000 – and a hamper of groceries from one of the famous shops in London!

The Tontine Club

HARRY RICHARDS

*Money – or rather the lack of it – often causes problems as
Christmas approaches. Fortunately, however, it is very unusual
indeed for money problems to have the tragic outcome they did in
this sad story recalled by Harry Richards, who was a lad of
about twelve at the time.*

Ifton Heath is a small village just a few miles from the Welsh
border. In the 1920s it consisted of a few miners' cottages, the
colliery and one or two outlying farms. Most of the men
worked in the pit and the 1926 strike had brought very hard
times to almost everyone in the village.

The majority of the miners contributed a few pennies every
week to a Tontine Club. In return they would be entitled to a
few shillings' sick pay per week if they were off work. In those
days, most people earned only a small wage and many had
large families. The club money was a lifeline in hard times.

If the club had any surplus funds at the end of the year,
these would be shared equally among the members and paid
out at Christmas time. The less sickness there had been
during the year, of course, the bigger the payment for each
member at Christmas but at the most we would collect £1 or
perhaps 25 shillings. In those days, however, that was
considered a formidable sum.

The pay-out took place on a pre-arranged night at the local
pub. Although the men were the members of the club, it was

the usual practice for their wives to collect the money. The fear was, if the men collected the share-out, some of it would be spent on beer and as a result the men might oversleep the next morning and lose the next day's work. In the 1920s that was unthinkable so generally most miners drank only at the weekend.

On this occasion I went with my mother to draw the Tontine. The landlady of the pub, as usual, allowed us to wait in the living quarters because in those days women didn't go into pubs. We waited. Time passed. People came and went but there was no sign of the treasurer – or the pay-out. At first jokes were made about the delay but as time went on it became obvious that something was seriously wrong. Eventually the women, who had sat waiting for so long, accepted there would be no pay-out that night.

We left the pub very disappointed and next morning heard the grim news.

The body of the treasurer had been recovered from a pond about a mile from his home in the village. Apparently he had succumbed to temptation during the hard times the miners had experienced in the 1926 strike. There was no money for the Christmas pay-out and, rather than face his fellow men, he had taken his own life.

He was a very likeable fellow and his death was a great waste for what was really only a very small amount of money.

from

Shropshire Days and Shropshire Ways

SIMON EVANS

Author and postman Simon Evans settled in Cleobury Mortimer after the First World War, hoping that the pure country air would ease the effects of wartime contact with poison gas. His delivery round, which involved walking about eighteen miles each day, brought him into close contact with the local people and the countryside, which feature in much of his work. In 1938, when this piece was written, the post was still delivered on Christmas Day.

A peep into any post office, large or small, during the pressure of Christmas work makes it easy to believe that the time of the year has arrived when everybody remembers everybody. All around are stacks of bags ready for dispatch, stacks of bags waiting to be opened, desks heaped high with letters, troughs and hampers full of packets, tens of thousands of cards, letters and gifts.

What do post office people think about Christmas Day? Before Christmas arrives I have no doubt that almost all post

office workers are tired. For a week or more their hours have been increased and they have been working harder than usual. Telephonists, telegraphists, clerks, sorters and postmen – all post office people are, I think, very much the same as other people who make up the population of our towns and villages. Some are naturally happy and gay, others are anxious and care-worn, some are easily excited, others are quiet, perhaps even a little dour. All sorts and conditions of men and women are employed to keep the machinery of the post office and the millions of letters, packets and parcels moving smoothly and easily in the way they should go. At Christmas time their work is multiplied many, many times.

If we remember all this it seems rather thoughtless and scoffing, or at any rate to be laughing up one's sleeve, to wish, let us say, the morning postman a merry Christmas. Probably what he needs more than anything else is a long, long sleep. But a warm greeting and a cheerful face, a hearty handshake and good-humoured banter are always welcome, gaiety and good cheer are infectious.

Have you ever wondered what a postman who has weathered twenty or more Christmas days thinks about this role of Father Christmas which he is forced to play? I think that there are some of us who rather like it; others, I am sure, dislike it intensely and are more than pleased when normal working order is restored. For my part I often wonder what a free and lazy Christmas would be like.

While employed at a large head post office I worked through several Christmas rush periods; since I came to live in Shropshire I have seen eleven Christmas mornings in a small country post office and spent eleven Christmas days walking to farms and cottages in the valley of the Rea, always within sight of Titterstone Clee Hills.

Let people say what they will, I do not believe that the postman of today is as indifferent and careless of the messages

he carries as he was supposed to be in Cowper's day. In the opening stanza of Book IV of *The Task*, Cowper wrote:

> Here he comes, the herald of a noisy world,
> With spattered boots, strapp'd waist and frozen locks,
> News from all nations lumbering at his back.
> True to his charge the close pack'd load behind,
> Yet careless what he brings, his one concern
> Is to conduct it to the destined inn,
> And having dropp'd the expected bag – pass on.

No, today – in country places at any rate – the postman is a native of the countryside over which he travels. It might almost be said that the length of hill and dale which makes

Heavy snow at Arleston House – an 'uncommonly handsome' property near Wellington

the daily walk is, for him, his little world. Experience has taught him that those letters which are accepted only to be thrown carelessly aside, or looked into with an incurious air, are of little importance. He knows that, more often than not, good news is expected and the recipients are almost always anxious to read what will confirm their hopes; while letters containing bad news are, as a rule, accepted with some hesitation and suspicion; indeed, they are often turned over and over and examined as if there must be some mistake – but no, the name is right, the address is right. Courage! It may not be as bad as you thought.

Many years ago all letters were important; sealed and stamped, they were seldom written or received by people of what was termed the lower orders. Today letters are written and received by almost every man, woman and child. I sometimes wonder what percentage of these missives described as letters or correspondence really are 'letters'. Nowadays the Royal Mail is made up of football coupons by the million, sales catalogues, samples, invoices, bills, and a whole host of various items which might be described as second, third, or even fourth class, correspondence.

The time of the year to see smiles of satisfaction on the faces of men and women, to hear shrieks of joy and excited laughter among children, is at Christmas time. This is also the time of the year when the postman is sure to call and he is more welcome than ever, for he seems to have an unlimited supply of what the people want. Youngsters, dancing with joy, eager, hasty and happy, tear open envelopes and cut the string of parcels. Then they shout: 'One from Uncle Bill in New Zealand', 'One from Cousin Tom in India', 'One from Dick in the Air Force'. Aunts, uncles, cousins, nephews, nieces, school friends, old friends, young friends, Sue and Maud, Joe and Harry, they have all remembered.

This gladness, this all-round cheerfulness, helps to ease the

burden of the postman. To be loaded with good news and gifts for all, to be a messenger of joy and goodwill is not a bad job. This feast of good things carried by the postman at Christmas time is, perhaps, one reason why he is welcome through the whole twelve months, until Christmas comes again.

What would I do if I were free to do just as I wish this Christmas time? Well, on Christmas Eve I'd like to set out for a walk on the hills, ramble without haste or any set timetable. I'd call at an inn I know. I'd call at a cottage or two, and I'd hope and try to arrive home before dark. In the evening I'd read – there are so many books I want to read – and I think the walking and the reading would make me ready for bed fairly early.

On Christmas morning I'd like to lie in bed for an extra hour or two, simply because I've never been able to do so before. Then, after breakfast, I'd walk a little, but I'd be very careful to be back home in time to open the door when the postman knocked. This would reverse the picture, as it were, and I'm sure I'd enjoy doing it because in the past I've always been the man who gives the double knock.

How strange it would be to open the door and receive my own letters on Christmas morning. Yes, how strange it would be to sit before the fire and read my own letters in comfort, and, later on, to sit to my Christmas dinner when other people sit to theirs.

But this is just an idle fancy you'll say. Yes, it is. Ah, well, I'll work. And you? I hope the postman brings you all you want, but remember:

'At Christmas – play and make good cheer, For Christmas comes but once a year.'

from

Mare's Milk and Wild Honey

PETER DAVIES

*Looking back on his childhood at Little Ness in the 1930s and
'40s, Peter Davies writes with affection and nostalgia about
what were, obviously, happy times.*

Drama was sudden and nearly always sanguinary on our farm: castration, pig killing, calving, farrowing – and the plucking of the Christmas geese. Mother told me that as a young farmer's bride she had held the geese behind her while my father cut their throats. And now, as every year, when winter drew over us and darkness tried to shut us in, I came home one day to a miasma of singed feathers and a sense of desolation. (You don't have to see death on a farm, you can feel it: something is missing.) And under a cloud of feathers I found my mother snapping and stripping – the sound was like an elastoplast being torn away – first the wings and then the bodies of those fifteen-pound-weight ghosts of geese.

She had her old brown beret on, fluted like a jelly mould but dusted over with fluff. And an old mac that never saw the light of day, with a sack drawn over her knees. And on the sack were the orange feet of the goose spread out to one side;

on the other the head hung down with an accusing eye. The feathers floated aloft, securing themselves in every grey cobweb of the old barn, or, lighting, ran along the ground.

'Just tidy up those breasts for me – I have another two to do,' my mother said.

I rolled a piece of paper up and, setting it alight, I singed the pink and yellow stippled skin. The lantern, set swinging on a beam, exaggerated the cavernous bowels of the old building and through the tickling, feathered air we talked in clouds of steam.

'I've several wreaths to make tonight. . . .' Her furred-up eyes suggested that I should go and find some holly, moss and bits of baling wire. 'And you'll just catch the post if you go now. I've done the Christmas things. And shut the fowl up on your way or there are some will never roost again! And . . .'

I left her quilted, muffled like a ghost, too deep, too deft, too diligent, too practised to put off what could still be done that night.

A few days later my mother said, 'When you go to the wood see if you can find a Christmas tree. Not too big – just the top off one would do.'

I mentioned it to Florrie, who smiled beguilingly, and, with a saw beneath my coat, we two preternaturally old figures floated silently round the penumbra of the copse. We could just make out the shapes of pheasants and hear their wings soft-shuffle overhead. Indian-file, we penetrated the dark heart of the wood, Florrie leading soundlessly, I two steps behind. 'Here's one,' she lisped. 'Gi' me the saw!' And before I could focus she was halfway up the tree and sawing fast. Beneath a baleful moon, we dragged our timber back, fearful of whom we might meet.

My mother was delighted with the tree. 'Take it to school tomorrow,' she said. 'But tell Miss Hyles the donor wishes to remain anonymous.'

A Shropshire Christmas

The following Friday night, the little schoolroom lit with unaccustomed cheer, the audience gathered, neighbour Martin and the other landowners prominent in the front seats, the Christmas tree aglow, the hornpipe began. Our mothers were smiling wonderingly at Florrie's effervescent glee and india-rubber bones as up the mast she went again, then down, and heel-and-toe she climbed imaginary air, descended, backed, unrolled her arms, then hauling on the bowline, climbed aloft. She ravelled everybody in her india-rubber charms.

Miss Hyles, hand on heart at the piano after keeping pace with all these accelerations, thanked the unknown donor of the Christmas tree. . . .

Two nights before Christmas, Mother said, 'You and John can take this cake to Lizzie at The Shruggs.' Lizzie was our old washerwoman. She lived in an umbra of larch trees and bracken on the way to Nesscliff Hill. Dark was the only word for The Shruggs. You could hardly see inside the two-roomed house; but there was a fire with pots bubbling and brewing round the hearth, and cats and sepia photographs and a settle and rag rugs.

Outside there was a tin shed, frosted over, where Lizzie's husband kept two cows. 'Distant in time as Palestine,' said John. We were given a Christmas tree to take back. 'From under the hill,' said Lizzie, knowing that Mother liked her tree to come from there. And on the way back we worked out a poem:

> Distant in time as Palestine,
> Two shorthorn cows lay down
> In a buckled shed,
> Its split-larch frame
> With corrugated iron spread
> And fir trees stood around.
>
> And hessian sacks were stuffed in gaps
> And bale wire hung on hooks,

But contentedly
The cows lay down
From draught and dampness almost free
Though frost winked on the ground.

'Those cows live as well as their owners,' said John. 'Surprising though, how snug a cattle shed can be.'

'Bluedy 'ell,' said Billy [an evacuee staying with the family] when he realized that because Christmas Eve had fallen on Sunday it meant he would have to go to church on Monday as well.

'We used to have three services on a Sunday,' I said to calm him down. 'Now we have only two because of the black-out. Evensong used to be at six-thirty.'

'Sex-therty?' said Billy. 'Yeh must uv spent all dee in cherch!'

'Just think,' I said, 'no Litany! And numbers fifty-nine and sixty-two!'

'What's sexty-two?'

' "While shepherds watched".'

'"Their ternip tops. . . . " 'Shall I sing yeh the Livapule varesion?'

We spent the evening dressing the Christmas tree with tinsel and clip-on candles and putting the decorations up. Sleep never came easily to me in the attic; and Father Christmas, I noticed, smoked the same Players cigarettes as last year, still coughed, but spent less time on her rounds. In the morning we found our stockings were pillow-cases and they contained not chocolate watches and tangerines or sugar mice but *White Fang* and a lambsfoot knife for John, *Tales of a Log Cabin* and a brummock (billhook) for Billy, and a set of mathematical instruments and Clementi's *Gradus Ad Parnassum* for me. For the girls there were *Little Women* and *Little Men* bulked up with materials for knitting, sewing and making wool rugs.

'Bluedy 'ell,' said Billy, inspecting his brummock. 'What's this?'

'A brummock.'

'Well, what's it foor?'

'For chopping sticks!' Billy, always reluctant to do his share, was guided to the Yule log in the shed.

'Look sharp!' called Mother. 'You'll need to get ready for church.'

'Christians, awake! Salute the happy morn . . .'

The church, of course, was a picture: the lid of the font was lapped with cloth as white as snow and ringed with berried holly, blood-bright red; the little thatched crib smelt of hay and candle wax, and the figures, brought, someone said, from Jerusalem, had been adoringly placed in exactly the same positions, in order, as last year.

Beagle Broadcast

JACK IVESTER LLOYD

Nearly forty years have passed, and much has changed, since Jack Ivester Lloyd wrote this description of a Boxing Day meet of the Shropshire Beagles. At the time Jack was writing about a county he only knew as a visitor. A few years later, however, fate and his family obliged him to leave his Bedfordshire base and become, by adoption, 'a proud Salopian' – and a great friend and mentor of the Shropshire Beagles.

One of the advantages of a writer's trade is that, sometimes, he gets paid for enjoying himself! I recognized one of these occasions on its way when Godfrey Baseley, the BBC producer, rang me up and said 'Jack, I want you to come to Much Wenlock in Shropshire, have a day's beagling, and do a broadcast on it afterwards. Oh, and you can bring your wife.' He added that there was one snag. The beagling and the broadcast would take place on Boxing Day, so we would have to travel on Christmas evening. What of it? I would walk to Cape Wrath for a day's beagling – that is, provided that I was not expected to do it in one day.

The Passenger Office at Euston informed me that there were trains which would carry us as far as Wellington, but no farther, and that we must change at Stafford. So we arranged a taxi to meet us at Wellington. Holiday travel can be a dreary business, but we boarded the evening train in high spirits. Audrey, with her usual forethought, had packed food and a drop o' summat. Apparently there was only one other passenger, a young WAAF going on leave, and, although she helped to brighten our journey, she spoiled the illusion that this train was 'our special'.

At Stafford, a cheerful porter opened the door, carried our bag, and in several other ways treated us to those courtesies which we felt we deserved as lone Christmas travellers, if for no other reason. But . . . 'Train to Wellington? Not tonight, sir! No, nor tomorrow, either!'

My first instinct was to laugh, but Audrey recognized the symptoms and kicked me hard on the shins. So, instead of laughing, I waggled my whiskers, took a deep breath and barked 'What? Here am I, booked to give an important broadcast from Much Wenlock tomorrow, and you tell me that there is no train? What will the BBC think of you – and what will the public think of British Railways, eh? Fetch the station master.' I was going to add 'fetch the mayor', but the strain of keeping a straight face was becoming too great.

Snow on Wenlock Edge in January 1973

I am sure that my tirade had nothing to do with the fact that the station staff were most helpful – after all, they were not responsible for running the trains – especially that nice, cheerful porter. He telephoned Much Wenlock and stopped the car which was going to meet us at Wellington; he found another taxi with an owner who was willing to drive us for more than thirty miles on this Christmas night. This driver was also a cheerful man and he grinned as he told us that, although he had never been to Much Wenlock, he was confident that we would eventually arrive there. And that we did, even though we traversed half the by-roads of Shropshire and climbed the Wrekin three times on the way – or so it seemed.

We awoke to a clear, frosty morning and, as we ate breakfast in the Gaskell Arms, we told ourselves that we were real early-morning people. But we were not so early as

Godfrey Baseley who walked in a few minutes later, having motored from Bromsgrove over icy roads. He soon had us at Collaughton Farm, where Bill Milner and his charming wife were welcoming what appeared to be half the BBC technical staff, as well as ourselves and others who were to take part in the broadcast.

I was enjoying the warmth of the Milner's fire, to say nothing of their rum and coffee, when Godfrey reminded us that, if we really meant to go beagling, we had better start right away. Mrs Phil Drabble decided to come out with the beagles, too; what is more, she drove us to the meet, ran well all day, and brought us back to the farm in the evening.

There is, of course, always a crowd at a Boxing Day meet of hounds. Some people call it 'going to the meet', others 'going to look at hounds' but, to the regular followers, it is 'going hunting', and from these terms it is possible to judge how far and how fast people mean to travel. I soon discovered that most of those who had turned up at The Windmill, on the Shrewsbury–Welshpool road, that day were 'going hunting'.

When Major George Leake moved off with that active, useful-looking pack of beagles, he took them to the northern side of the ridge, and, as we entered a big, sloping field of plough, I realized that I was gazing upon what well may have been the loveliest view of England which I have ever seen. In front of us was the sweep of the wide Severn Valley, a patchwork of brown and green fields with narrow strips of silver where the frost lay gleaming under the hedgerows. Beyond the valley rose ranges of hills, each a little higher than the range in front, and the skyline was the Welsh mountains, snow-capped and shining in the light of the sun which shone all day.

It was the sun and the lingering frost which, pleasing though they were to the senses, hampered hunting conditions and, although a brace of hares were soon on the move, hounds

could hunt only slowly. Now there are times when I enjoy slow hunting and this was one of them, for it gave me an opportunity of appreciating the thorough way in which those hounds worked and the patience of their huntsman. It also allowed me time for getting to know some of the other followers. Two were friends from the Old Berkeley country, Tony Wilkinson and his wife. Tony, who is a native of Shropshire, was carrying a whip on this day, as he does regularly with the Old Berkeley Beagles. Also out, and going well, was Victor Threadgold, huntsman to the Border Counties Otterhounds.

We crossed the road, we ran past the pig farm, and several times hounds took the line through the spinney on the hillside just below The Windmill, but they never got on good terms with either of these hares.

At last, after a longish check near the spinney, George Leake lifted his hounds and took them over the hill. Here was

'Hounds took the line through the spinney . . . '

less frost, more grassland, and better scenting conditions. A fresh hare got up in the next field to The Windmill and hounds really showed the stuff of which they were made. We splashed through wet furrows, we scrambled over full ditches, and ever the cry of the pack led us on. Three times that hare led us in a very wide circle and, when going round for the third time, she must have discovered that speed alone would not save her scut. She tried turning short, but, after only a brief check, hounds swung back on her line. She ran the hedgerows – and was viewed as she broke from one. Then she took a course through a herd of cattle, but even their foil did not shake off the eager pack. So she entered a thick woodland, only to be pushed through by hounds which were too close to allow her to clap.

With each moment, the sun was sinking nearer to the golden peaks and ridges of the mountains in the westward, and light was fading. There was but a short space of daylight left in which that hare could be caught or given best. My wife viewed her from the road as she went over the hill and so gained the northern slope where there was little scent. On that brown hillside, where the wind was cold and the rime had lain all day, hounds puzzled out her line, yard by yard. And there, as darkness fell, the hare pulled off that mysterious trick which so many others before her have accomplished – she disappeared.

As we changed our shoes and stockings in the near-darkness, Audrey reminded me that we had to broadcast from Collaughton Farm that evening. We hurried. Once again the roads were coated with ice but that worried Mrs Phil Drabble, who was driving, not a jot.

Of the many times that I have talked over the radio, this occasion will surely be the most memorable. The microphone, set up in the drawing-room of that delightful farmhouse, the overwhelming hospitality of the Milners, the happy, warm-

hearted company with their dogs of many kinds, Godfrey's breezy entrance when the red light came on, the account of her day with the Wheatland Foxhounds given by that grand naturalist and sportswoman, Miss Frances Pitt, Frank Waterhouse talking about his pike fishing and Phil Drabble about his rabbitting.

What did I talk about? Beagling, of course! What did I say about it? I do not remember. As for Audrey, she chipped in with the remark that cleaning beagling kit is almost a whole-time job with her.

Taken all round, it was a wonderful Boxing Day.

The Bells of Shropshire

These rhymes are said to be several centuries old. Whatever the truth of that, they have certainly been learnt by many generations of Shropshire schoolchildren.

A nut and a kernel,
Say the bells of Acton Burnell,
A pudding in the pot,
Say the bells of Acton Scott.
Pitch 'em and patch 'em,
Say the bells of Old Atcham.
Under and over,

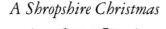

Say the bells of Condover,
An old lump of wood,
Say the bells of Leebotwood.
Three crows on a tree,
Say the bells of Oswestry.
Buttermilk and whey
Say the bells of Hopesay.
Roast beef and be merry,
Say the bells of Shrewsbury.
A new-born baby,
Say the bells of St Mary.

The Farmer's Christmas

LYN BRIGGS

Turn off any of the main Shropshire thoroughfares and within a few miles you will find yourself in a quiet country lane. The road will be narrow and it is likely to have high hedges of hawthorn, holly or blackthorn. If your visit is in winter, it is possible you will see the hedge-layer at work on the dormant branches. He will trim out any lanky, useless growth and cut part-way through good, strong branches to lay them almost horizontal.

Before the advent of barbed wire, his work was essential to

make the hedge stock-proof and it is still important if the bottom of the hedge is not to become thin and gappy. Return in spring if you want to judge how well the job has been done. The branches which were nicked and laid horizontally should now be sprouting new growth. If they are dead, the hedge-layer has failed miserably in his task.

Shropshire is a county of agricultural contrasts. The hills, of which there are many, are alive with sheep. In the north, around Ellesmere, there were once more dairy cows per acre than anywhere else in the world. To the east of the county is good grain land. A winter visitor might well see naked, brown fields, where sugar beet has recently been lifted from the ground by big machines. There is a beet processing factory at Allscott, near Shrewsbury and 'the campaign', as they call the time they are prepared to accept loads of beet for processing into sugar, finishes probably in late January.

'Geese gobbling and grazing away the last few weeks before Christmas'

During that time the processor works non-stop – even on Christmas Day.

The rest of the harvest should be stored in barns or silos long before the warm golden days of autumn give way to the frost and fogs of winter.

By Christmas, many corn fields, worked and sown in what farmers call 'the back-end' of the year, are already covered with the young green shoots of next year's harvest.

Shropshire meadows provide bed and board for thousands of Welsh sheep down from the hills to spend winter in a softer climate. They will return in early spring ready for lambing, which starts late in the hill country. In milder areas the first lambs may well be born at Christmas time and the shepherd will watch his flock anxiously, feeding the ewes with great care to prepare them for motherhood.

At one time almost every farm kept a few poultry or geese for Christmas to provide welcome extra cash at an expensive time of the year. The practice is less common now and new European Community regulations may eventually stop all but large scale production. It is still possible to see a farmyard flock of geese gobbling and grazing away the last few weeks before Christmas.

As the festivities approach, foresters leave off their regular work to cut or dig Christmas trees. If you meet a truck piled high with trees or holly, the chances are it is on its way to the famous Christmas auction just across the county border at Tenbury Wells.

Farmers too have special preparations to make if they want to show well-groomed cattle, which will do credit to their herd, at the local primestock show.

Six o'clock on Christmas morning, the farmer's alarm rings – just as it does on any other morning. He has stock to feed and probably cows to milk. Then he can enjoy his Christmas lunch and put his feet up for a few hours before the evening milking and feeding.

Times have changed and animal husbandry is too scientific now for the farmer to follow the old tradition of double rations for the animals on Christmas morning. Gone too is the old belief that if you crept out to the cattle shed at midnight on Christmas Eve you would see the animals kneeling as they once did for the baby Jesus.

But it is possible that, when the shepherd drags himself from his whisky and warm fireside out into the sharp December evening to check his ewes, he will find at least one has marked the special day by presenting him with a newborn lamb or two.

Food Fit for a Festival

MEG PYBUS

Good quality, tasty food has always been a priority in most Shropshire homes – especially at Christmas – as this piece, written by an authority on food in the county, explains.

A modern Shropshire family can enjoy their food on Christmas Day a few hours after a trip to their local supermarket. But, in bygone times, much larger families lived mainly off the land and bought, and maybe sold, their produce in the local market. Whether rich or poor they spent

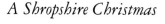
many more hours, weeks and months preparing for the highlight of their year.

If one walked or rode into a typical Shropshire town just before Christmas, the displays of food were much more obvious. In the absence of strict hygiene regulations, the shopkeepers used the outside of their shops to create colourful and attractive displays. Geese, game and rabbits hung upside down outside the poulterers. At the greengrocers nets of melons were suspended amongst the holly and mistletoe. Below were barrels of grapes, pomegranates, oranges and tangerines, boxes of apples, pears and pineapples. The grocers decorated their windows with chains of hams and bacon. They weighed and packed their goods in October and made up their own packets of dried fruit, blended Indian and China teas (said to suit the local water) and wrapped their butter and lard.

The carriage trade was courted. Upstairs or at the back of the shop there was an elaborate display room for special customers. If you lived in a country house, or at the hall, a mobile display van came to you.

'The brawn season has commenced,' announced Elizabeth Hand, brawn maker to the Queen, in the *Shrewsbury Chronicle* of December 1848. She also offered boar's head 'properly cured and ornamented for the table' from her premises in Double Butchers Row, and thanked 'her favoured customers of the gentry and nobility for their patronage'. The Christmas brawn, made from the pig's head and foreparts, had been popular since feudal times. At feasts, the lacquered and piped boar's head with an orange in its mouth was carried in on a large platter.

The place of the pig at Christmas is centuries old: 21 December is St Thomas' day, and conveniently he is the patron saint of brewing, baking and pig-killing.

In Shropshire, pigs fattened on acorns, beech mast or

Christmas market about 1903 outside Mr Jim Wood's shop in
Market Drayton

chestnuts would provide the small farmer with salted pork,
bacon and lard. It was said that you ate every part of the pig –
except his squeak. Flitches of bacon were rubbed with salt and
brown sugar or treacle and preserved with hams and pork for
six weeks or more in large earthenware pots of brine. The
joint of pork may have satisfied the cottager but, for the lord
of the manor in medieval times, a prime ox had to be killed to
provide the baron of beef. Traditional roast beef is still
preferred at Christmas by some Shropshire families.

A goose was often a significant part of many Shropshire
Christmas meals. When left to roam geese could be fattened
cheaply.

An eighty-year-old Shropshire woman remembers the
arrival of the waggoner on a dark December morning. 'He

caught, weighed and tied each goose's wings and feet before taking mother on the cart to market. The geese were then laid out on straw on the ground for mother to sell.'

In the kitchen, cooks and kitchen maids were busy. Sometime in October numerous puddings were stirred with a wish, then boiled in calico tied up like old purse bags. These, and the silver trinkets put inside, were a reminder of St Nicholas' generosity. The puddings were boiled for eight hours in the wash copper.

Plum puddings were once made with plums and earlier in the fifteenth century contained pieces of beef. Large earthenware steins were packed with minced meat in readiness for pie-making on Christmas Eve. The mince pies we eat today have little in common with the sixteenth-century 'pyes of mutton or beefe minced and mixed with shredded suet, seasoned with cloves, mace, pepper, saffron, raisins, currants and prunes'.

The heavy medieval cakes often weighed twenty lb or more but seemed light in comparison to the great sixty-four lb Christmas cake made at the Royal Salop Infirmary during the First World War.

Shropshire folk are noted for their hospitality and charity. Generous landowners provided joints of beef and pork for their tenants long before the welfare state. St Thomas' Day (21 December) was considered alms-giving day. Farmers donated sacks of wheat to the poor, and from this frumenty, the nutritious cereal pottage was made for a Christmas treat.

Even in this century, in the village of Cheswardine, in the north of the county, a baker remembers weighing out fourteen lb of flour to 'anyone who has less than an acre or a cow'. People arrived with pillow slips and sacks. Some parochial church charities donated loaves of bread.

After church on Christmas Day all the family gathered around the dining-room table to watch father carve the goose,

scoop out the sage and onion stuffing and hand around the apple sauce. The younger members may have found the brandy-laden Christmas pudding, brandy sauce, mince pies, stilton and port a little too rich and preferred the light egg custards.

The men probably lingered with the port and the women and children retired to the drawing-room yule-log fire. The servants cleared and washed up, then prepared the evening table of numerous cold meats, pork pie, brawn, jellies and pickles, trifle, gingerbread, macaroons and other sweetmeats.

After evensong they ate their own simpler version of Christmas dinner and relaxed over their specially made beer and home-made wines. At the end of a long, exhausting period, a holiday on Boxing Day may have been the beginning of a few days' well-earned rest.

Putting on a Show

LYN BRIGGS

By November rehearsals are in full swing throughout the county, as children and grown-ups — many talented amateurs and a few hardened professionals — prepare the Christmas entertainment. The performers of the 1990s are following a proud tradition, for not every county can claim links with two of the best pantomime stories, as well as being the home county of the man credited with introducing pantomime to England! All three claims are somewhat light on facts, but we'll not let that ruin a good story!

John Weaver, the Shrewsbury-born dancing master with a national reputation, can certainly be said to have produced the first 'pantomime' performed in England. The production was at London's Drury Lane Theatre in 1702 and in it, 'dancing, action and motion' were used to tell the story. It was not a success and Weaver's second attempt, some years later, also flopped.

As with so many things, someone else took up and developed the idea. That man was John Rich. He added Harlequin, a character from Italian Commedia dell' Arte and pantomime was here to stay.

A Shropshire man had played a part in its conception but, I suspect John Weaver, who took dance very seriously, was bitterly disappointed with the way his idea was developed. He continued to work for a more 'refined and graceful form of presentation' but, as a professional, he knew he must give his audience what they wanted – and would, therefore, pay to see. He composed comic interludes for a 1725 Drury Lane production and in 1728 took the part of the clown in the same production.

John Weaver always maintained strong links with Shrewsbury. He had dance pupils in the town, who gave a performance of 'The Judgement of Paris', a 'new Pantomime Entertainment' which had first been produced at Drury Lane in 1733. Weaver died in 1760 in Shrewsbury and is buried in Old St Chad's Church.

Shropshire's other connections with pantomime centre on the Oswestry area. Whittington proudly claims to be the birthplace of Sir Richard Whittington, thrice Lord Mayor of London and, with his cat, star of countless pantomimes.

Babbinswood, just up the road, was said by some to have been the site of the dreadful deeds which inspired the tale of Babes in the Wood. Nonsense, others say. There was a wicked murder in 1590 of a child of five for his inheritance, for which

no less than five people – four of them relatives of the victim – were executed. But that was at Knockin on the heath and had nothing to do with babies or woods!

Christmas entertainment in Shropshire doesn't just revolve around the slap and tickle of pantomimes. Back in the 1880s *Eddowes' Journal* was respectfully drawing its readers' attention to the arrangements at the Theatre Royal (Shrewsbury) for the Christmas season because 'it is only under very special circumstances that a company such as Mrs Chippendale's, the members of which are usually, when in the provinces, to be found attracting large audiences at Liverpool, Manchester or other large cities, could be engaged for a brief campaign in Shrewsbury'. The 'rare intellectual treat' they were to offer was *She Stoops to Conquer* and *Black-eyed Susan*.

Theatre-lovers in the town today will say little has changed, except that Shrewsbury no longer has a purpose-built theatre.

Modern parents, who miss the school Christmas concert at their peril, will sympathize with the mothers and fathers of Miss Barke's young pupils from Kingston House who took over the reading room at the Music Hall in Shrewsbury for their Christmas Entertainment one afternoon just before Christmas 1885. The programme survives and reveals that as well as a play – *Winter Blossoms* – the little dears (aged between five and twelve) gave twenty-five recitations, six piano solos and a duet. For good measure, the school's good conduct awards were also presented during what must have been a lengthy afternoon.

The local paper, of course, reported the event at some length. The writer was very impressed and Daisy Harrison (two recitations and a piano solo) earned a special mention for her performance of 'Curfew must not ring tonight' which 'reflected especial credit upon her and considerable surprise was manifested at her perfectly natural demeanour and

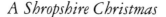

expression of feeling whilst reciting this, for a child, somewhat difficult piece'.

The reporter did have one slight criticism of the event. The presence of a large gathering of parents and friends made the room 'almost uncomfortably packed'.

In village halls and school assembly rooms throughout the county this year, as ever, popular Christmas shows will no doubt still be packing them in!

A Special Visitor

GEOFF ELSON

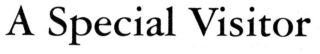

Christmas was coming and it wasn't easy for a young lad to cope with life in a children's home – but a special visitor and an unexpected treat certainly helped.

I was born and grew up in Whitchurch, one of a family of nine children. It can't have been easy for Mum and Dad to feed and clothe us all and, if I brought home a little extra, no questions were asked.

Sometimes I pestered Old Man Bradbury to let me clean his butcher's shop floor and put down fresh sawdust in return for a breast of mutton for Sunday lunch.

Occasionally I stole food which is how, when I was about ten years old, I got into trouble with the police, had to go to court and found myself in care in the Mount Children's Home in Wellington. I was a brave lad for my age but when I first

went there I was frightened. The rules had to be obeyed and those in charge were more strict than kind.

It was one of those years in the 1960s when you really knew it was winter. There had been ice, frost and snow – and there was the promise of more to come – when, not long before Christmas, I had a letter from my Dad. He was going to come and see me on Saturday for the first time since I had been put in the home.

The letter came on a Wednesday or Thursday. It wasn't much of a letter. Dad's never were. Just a quick note. By Friday I was so excited that I couldn't sleep. I was first at breakfast on Saturday morning and had my chores finished by 10 a.m. Then I went and sat in the 'quiet room' because from there I could see down the drive and just catch a glimpse of the top of the Midland Red buses as they pulled up at the shelter. I couldn't see who got off them though. Seven, eight, nine buses I counted. Still no sign of Dad. When lunchtime came, I didn't want to eat anything but I knew there would be trouble if I didn't clear my plate, so I forced it down. I was back in the quiet room watching the buses and the driveway by 1 p.m.

By 4 p.m. I'd sort of given up. Dad was always in The Lamb in Whitchurch by 7 p.m. on a Saturday. Finally, just before teatime, Mr Stokes (head of the home) came and told me that Dad had phoned. He'd missed his connection in Shrewsbury.

A few days later there was another letter from Dad with a 10s note saying he'd try to get here the next weekend. But during that long wait in the quiet room I'd lost my trust in him.

The next Saturday morning I was back in my spot by the window in the quiet room waiting, but not really believing he would come, so not daring to get excited. After all it was just a few days before Christmas and it was snowing heavily.

Shropshire countryside: beautiful whatever the weather

About 2.30 p.m. a bus pulled up and a few moments later a tall chap, a bit stooped with arthritis, started to walk up the drive. I looked twice to make sure, then nipped through the laundry and out of the back door. On the driveway I stopped. I'd planned to run and hug him but now I wasn't sure. I didn't want to be all soppy, so I stood still and waited to shake his hand like a little gentleman.

We went back into the quiet room and talked for a while. Dad wanted to know what I'd done with the 10*s*. Most of it was gone. I'd bought a case, and some pencils, off the market and written 'from Dad' on the inside. Then I told him about the burgundy cartridge pen which I'd seen in W.H. Smith's. It was 5*s* and I'd set my heart on it.

Dad was sharp. Money was tight, he explained, and I'd already had 10s and the bag of sweets he'd just given me. He'd some shopping to do for Mum on the way home and there was no money to spare. But I was wise for my age and thought it more likely he was thinking about his Saturday ale money!

We set out to walk up the town through snow that was already over my wellingtons. When we passed Smith's I mentioned the pen, got a sharp reply and shed one or two tears.

On the way back, Dad asked me to wait outside when we got to Smith's, while he went in. I didn't hold out much hope for the pen. I was sure he'd buy me a cheap biro and was feeling pretty miserable, especially as it was getting close to teatime and I would be in big trouble if we were late back.

When he came out, we hurried as quickly as we could, through thick snow. After tea, just before Dad left, we went back to the quiet room to say goodbye. He took a packet from his pocket and handed it to me. I opened it and inside was the burgundy pen. Suddenly the idea of spending Christmas in the home didn't seem so bad after all. My Dad must love me. He'd come all the way from Whitchurch, through thick snow, just to see me – and he'd bought me that wonderful pen.

Christmas Present

LYN BRIGGS

'Christmas', a certain cynic said, 'is about buying presents they won't appreciate, for people you don't like, with money you can't spare.' That statement may be extreme, but it contains an ominous element of truth. The simple pleasures of Christmas seem to have been misplaced in Shropshire, just as much as they have in the rest of the country.

From the moment the first Christmas card catalogue arrives in the post – usually about August – a desperate need to spend money sets in to celebrate the arrival, in a Bethlehem cattle-shed, of a boy child born to a carpenter and his lady. By October the shops have been decorated with colour coordinated tinsel and the serious build-up to Christmas is underway. Stroll through Telford's impressive all-covered shopping centre, or wander around Shrewsbury's or Ludlow's historic streets, and piped carols follow you everywhere.

Nine to five, six days a week is nowhere near enough time to buy all that must be bought, so we have late night shopping one or two nights a week and – a recent blessing – Sunday opening.

Why the preparations take so long is one of the few remaining mysteries of the festive season. In theory, at least, it should be possible – but admittedly expensive – to buy all that is necessary by the trolley-full, in one, or perhaps two, swoops on the local supermarket.

But it just does not work out like that. Spoilt for choice, in the wonderful selection of Shropshire shops, it is tempting to

*If Father Christmas had Aladdin's Lamp
he could hardly command a more wonderful
assortment of Toys and Gifts for Children
of all ages than is to be seen at* =====

Della Porta's
Shrewsbury

EXCITING TOYS FOR CHILDREN.

'Della Porta's . . . sold almost everything . . . with style, courtesy
and, seemingly, all the time in the world'

dally for days choosing just one present. This is why it is possible to start Christmas shopping in October and still be found fighting through the crowds on that desperate last Saturday. For those with nerves of steel, Christmas Eve is often the quietest shopping day in December in many Shropshire towns and, of course, the January sales are in full swing by then in at least some shops.

The art (or is it a science?) of shopping has changed over the years in Shropshire. We no longer have the wonderful department stores, such as Della Porta's in Shrewsbury, which sold almost everything and did so with style, courtesy and, seemingly, all the time in the world. Items for sale are no longer neatly tucked away in cabinets of glass-fronted drawers, from which prim assistants would, on request, show you what was available.

Also gone is the lady or gentleman who handled all money matters from a special booth, originally using tramways across the ceiling to shuttle money and receipts around the larger shops. The system of just one person handling all payments, which had much to recommend it, has always been popular in Shropshire and I don't doubt there are still shops that use it. There were at least two doing so in Shrewsbury until very recently.

Although the ways of shopping have changed in Shropshire, as they have nationwide, and the county can boast of the presence of all the major chain stores and has 'out-of-town' retail parks, it is fortunate still to have many excellent specialist shops. If you have anything from a stamp collection to a stuffed parrot on your Christmas shopping list, it is possible to buy it without leaving the county.

Markets still flourish in Shropshire and most towns – even the small ones – hold one each week. At Christmas people travel from miles around to buy provisions from the extensive street market at Market Drayton, where only a favoured few stalls are under-cover, and the rest take their chances in the best – and the worst – of the weather.

The legendary market on the Bailey Head at Oswestry and the ancient one at Wellington also pull in the crowds. They are popular because they offer good quality, particularly for food, and that other great love of all Shropshire people – bargains!

New Year's Eve

A.E. HOUSMAN

From the author of A Shropshire Lad *comes this thought-provoking piece marking the end of one year, and the beginning of the next.*

The end of the year fell chilly
Between a moon and a moon;
Through the twilight shrilly
The bells rang, ringing no tune.

The windows stained with story,
The walls with miracles scored,
Were hidden from gloom and glory
Filling the house of the Lord.

Arch and aisle and rafter
And roof-tree dizzily high
Were full of weeping and laughter
And song and saying good-bye.

A Shropshire Christmas

There stood in the holy places
A multitude none could name,
Ranks of dreadful faces
Flaming, transfigured in flame.

Crown and tiar and mitre
Were starry with gold and gem;
Christmas never was whiter
Than fear on the face of them.

In aisles that emperors vaulted
For a faith the world confessed,
Abasing the Host exalted,
They worshipped towards the west.

They brought with laughter oblation;
They prayed, not bowing the head;
They made without tear lamentation,
And rendered me answer and said:

'O thou that seest our sorrow,
It fares with us even thus:
Today we are gods, tomorrow
Hell have mercy on us.

'Lo, morning over our border
From out of the west comes cold;
Down ruins the ancient order
And empire builded of old.

'Our house at even is queenly
With psalm and censers alight:
Look though never so keenly
Thou shalt not find us tonight.

143

'We are come to the end appointed
With sands not many to run;
Divinities disanointed
And kings whose kingdom is done.

'The peoples knelt down at our portal,
All kindreds under the sky;
We were gods and implored and immortal
Once; and today we die.'

They turned them again to their praying,
They worshipped and took no rest
Singing old tunes and saying
'We have seen his star in the west.'

Old tunes of the sacred psalters,
Set to wild farewells;
And I left them there at their altars
Ringing their own dead knells.

And Finally . . .

*It would seem wrong to conclude this jaunt through Christmas
in Shropshire without mentioning that . . .*

On Christmas Day 1572, two houses which were supported
by beams across the navigation arch of the English or Stone
Bridge (in Shrewsbury) fell into the river because the ends of

the timbers were decayed. Fortunately all the occupants were at church at the time and therefore no one was hurt!

From The History of Myddle, *Richard Gough (writing in 1701)*

Parish Clarks. The first that I remember was Will. Hunt, a person very fitt for the place, as to his reading and singing with a clear and audible voice; but for his writeing I can say nothing. Hee commonly kept a petty schoole in Myddle. There was a custom in his time, that upon Christmas day, in the afternoone after divine service, and when the minister was gone out of the churche, the clarke should sing a Christmas carroll in the churche, which I have heard this Will. Hunt doe, being assisted by old Mr Richard Gitting, who bore a base exceedingly well.

From the Gentleman's Magazine *for 1790, regarding yule-logs*

The fire of these logs of wood, which were in fact great trees, may be collected from hence; that, in the time of the Civil Wars of the last century, Captain Hosier (I suppose of the Berwick family) burnt the house of Mr Barker, of Haghmond [*sic*] Abbey, near Shrewsbury, by setting fire to the yule-log. In the confusion occasioned by this event, Mr B. laid a bag of money in a place where a stone fell upon it, and concealed it. It was suspected that a servant in the family, one Maddocks, had stolen it, and he was in consequence discharged. This man lived to a very great age; and before he died, his reputation was cleared by the money being discovered. (From the information of an old lady.)

From the Parish Register at Melverley, dated a few days before Christmas 1766. (Perhaps preparations for Christmas explain the obvious haste and good spirits!)

This morning I have put a Tye
No man could put it faster,
'Tween Matthew Dodd, the man of God
And modest Nelly Foster.
John Lewis, Clk.

In January 1891 the weather was 'exceedingly trying and severe'. The Rivers Teme and Corve were frozen, and heavy falls of snow allowed tobogganing – 'a novelty' in Shrewsbury as reported in the Shrewsbury Chronicle:

We question much whether the central walk of our beautiful Quarry has ever been made the scene of so much enjoyment and excitement as it has in the past week. Some hundreds of people have watched the career of the venturesome tobogganists and amusing in the extreme has it been to witness the erratic locomotion of some of the strange 'craft' that have appeared on the well-worn slide. A capital track was made from the top to the bottom of the central avenue, and as many as 15 or 20 toboggans have been seen swiftly gliding down the track at the same time at the imminent risk sometimes of a grand collision and collapse.

The toboggans themselves were well worthy of an inspection. Some had evidently been turned out by skilful workmen, and were of excellent make and finish; others were less pretentious in their character and were intended for hard work rather than show; still more were of a very primitive design, and bore unmistakable signs of having at one time or another been portions of the useful bacon box or packing case.

Whatever vehicles, however, the tobogganists possessed, one and all, old and young – ladies as well as gentlemen – and rich and poor alike, immensely enjoyed the fun so unexpectedly afforded them.

Sources and Acknowledgements

Thanks are due to the authors, their representatives, publishers, etc. for their kind permission to reproduce copyright material. The extract from *The Raven in the Foregate* by Ellis Peters is reprinted by permission of the author and Macmillan London Ltd. 'Dick Whittington's Probable Birthplace' by Fletcher Moss was published in *Pilgrimages to Old Homes Mostly on the Welsh Border*, published by the author and reprinted with acknowledgement to E.J. Morten. 'An Extraordinary Year' is an extract from the third volume of The Transactions of the Shropshire Archaeological and Historical Society and is reprinted with acknowledgement to the society. Special thanks to the society's chairman, James Lawson, for help clarifying the question of the 'green geese'. The explanations first appeared in 'Salopian Shreds and Patches' in *Eddowes' Journal*.

'Salopian Songs of Praise' by Gordon Ashman is printed by permission of the author. 'The Victorian Visitor' by Beryl Copsey appeared in *The Shropshire Magazine* in December 1986 and is reprinted by permission of the editor. The extract from the diaries of Hannah Cullwick is reprinted from an edition of the diaries edited by Liz Stanley, published by Virago Press (1984). It is reprinted by permission of the Master and Fellows of Trinity College, Cambridge and Virago Press Ltd. 'The Curmudgeons' Christmas' text and illustrations by Randolph Caldecott appeared in *The Graphic* (Dec. 1885) and is reprinted with acknowledgement to *The Illustrated London News*.

'A Very Different Christmas' by Rachael Iliffe is printed by permission of the Ironbridge Gorge Museum Trust. 'Family Life' by Rachel Jones and the letter from Edward German are the copyright of the Edward German Archive reproduced by permission. Thanks to Dr David Russell Hulme for permission to reprint material from the Edward German Archive.

'To Mother' by Mary Webb was printed in *The Collected Works of Mary*

Webb published by Jonathan Cape Ltd (1929) and is reprinted with acknowledgement to the estate of the author and the publishers. The extract from *A House That Was Loved* by Katherine Kenyon was published by Methuen (1941) and is reprinted by permission of Colonel J.F. Kenyon. 'Letters Home' by Wilfred Owen is the copyright of Oxford University Press (1967). Reprinted from Wilfred Owen: *Collected Letters*, edited by Harold Owen and John Bell (1967) by permission of Oxford University Press. The extract from *Burlton Village* by Marjorie Jones was first published by the author (1989) and is reprinted by her permission. The extract from *Memories of Clun* by Ronald K. Moore, first published by Shropshire Books, is reprinted by permission of the author and Shropshire Books. 'Recollections of the Old Welsh Frankton Carol Singers' by Tom Borderer appeared in *The Shropshire Magazine* in December 1957, and 'Sam Evans' Christmas Carol' by E.V. Bayne in the same publication in December 1956. Both pieces are reprinted by permission of the editor of *The Shropshire Magazine.*

'Down Memory Lane' by W.L.M. Francis, 'The Tontine Club' by Harry Richards and 'A Special Visitor' by Geoff Elson were written in collaboration with Lyn Briggs.

The extract from *Shropshire Days and Shropshire Ways* by Simon Evans, published by Heath Cranton Ltd (1938) is reprinted with acknowledgement to the estate of the author and thanks to Dr Mark Baldwin, Cleobury Mortimer, expert on, and supplier of, the works of Simon Evans. The extract from *Mares Milk and Wild Honey* by Peter Davies, published by André Deutsch (1987) is reprinted by permission of the author and André Deutsch. 'Beagle Broadcast' by J. Ivester Lloyd first appeared in *The Shooting Times* and *Country Magazine* (22 January 1954) and is reprinted by permission of the editor of that magazine and Delphine Hulme. 'Food Fit for a Festival' by Meg Pybus is printed by permission of the author. 'New Year's Eve' by A.E. Housman, published by Jonathan Cape (1939) is reprinted with acknowledgement to the estate of the author and Jonathan Cape Ltd.

Many people have helped me to compile this book. I am very grateful to them all but here I would like to record my special thanks to: staff at Shropshire Libraries, particularly at the Records and Research Unit at Castle Gates; Gordon Dickins; Delia Harvey; Delphine Hulme – and George and John Briggs.

Picture Credits

Title page, pp. 28, 47, 48, 49, 74: Randolph Caldecott; pp. 3, 5, 37, 54, 57, 82, 93, 137: H.R. Savage, reproduced by kind permission of Helen Jones; p. 12: courtesy of Shropshire Newspapers Ltd; pp. 19, 45, 65, 111, 120: Records and Research Unit of Shropshire Leisure Services (pp. 91 and 92 courtesy of John Luther through the Records and Research Unit); p. 22: courtesy of Gordon Ashman; pp. 25, 51, 52, 78, 87: Ironbridge Gorge Museum Trust; pp. 25, 31, 33: courtesy of the Master and Fellows of Trinity College, Cambridge; p. 61: courtesy of the Edward German Archive; pp. 103, 105, 130: Drayton Civic Society; p. 122: courtesy of *The Shooting Times* and Delphine Hulme; p. 126: courtesy of W. Dodd.

I am very grateful to all those listed above for their permission to use photographs and illustrations to which they retain the rights.